Off-campus Library Services

Selected Readings from
Central Michigan University's
Off-campus Library Services
Conferences

Compiled and edited by
Barton M. Lessin

78667

The Scarecrow Press, Inc.
Metuchen, N.J., & London
1991

British Library Cataloguing-in-Publication data available

Library of Congress Cataloging-in-Publication Data

Off-campus library services : selected readings from Central Michigan
    University's Off-campus Library Services Conferences / compiled
    and edited by Barton M. Lessin.
         p.   cm.
      Includes bibliographical references and indexes.
      ISBN 0-8108-2512-0 (acid-free paper)
      1. Libraries, University and college--Congresses.   2. Libraries
    and students--Congresses.   3. University extension--Congresses.
    4. Distance education--Congresses.   5. Library extension--Con-
    gresses.   I. Lessin, Barton M.   II. Off-campus Library Services
    Conference.
    Z675.U50453   1991
    025.5'2777--dc20   91-38119

Printed on acid-free paper

To

John W. Weatherford

Emeritus Director of Libraries
Central Michigan University

and

Judy Lessin

How fortunate I am to have found
the needle in the haystack.

Table of Contents

Preface

A great many individuals participated in the development of this volume, some through their encouragement and others by their active participation in the Central Michigan University Libraries off-campus library program, the Off-campus Library Services Conference, or the conference proceedings.

First and foremost John Weatherford, Director Emeritus of the Central Michigan University Libraries, deserves my most sincere thanks. Without his guidance, encouragement, and enthusiasm there would never have been even one conference much less conference proceedings. Provost John Cantelon was an early supporter of the conference and served as one of its first featured speakers. His help is much appreciated.

Lacking Central Michigan University's commitment to off-campus adult education there would have been no reason to contemplate the kind of conference that this book represents. I owe a debt of gratitude to those members of the University's School of Extended Learning and its Institute for Personal and Career Development who consistently support efforts to provide quality off-campus library services. The Dean of the School of Extended Learning and the Directors of the Institute time and again demonstrate their dedication to off-campus library programming; Dr. John Yantis, Dr. Lawrence Murphy, and Dr. Robert Trullinger have all proven their support for these efforts. Dr. Trullinger deserves special mention here as he has made the off-campus library services program at C.M.U. a focus of academic and Institute excellence during his continuing term as director. Dr. Royce Breland was among the very first to recommend that the Central Michigan University off-campus library program be the focus of a conference. His confidence in the value of such a meeting provided needed encouragement. Dr. Richard Potter, who is represented in this volume, is another of the IPCD administrators who strongly supports the library program and the Off-campus Library Services Conference. Any number of Richard's creative ideas have been included within the concepts of the C.M.U. off-campus library support program and the conference which is a reflection of it.

The conference itself has always been a team effort with the C.M.U. regional librarians involved in planning and implementation. Monica

Collier, Maryhelen Garrett, Kelly Gordon, Jeneane Johanningmeier, Marcie Kingsley, Evelyn Leasher, Gloria Lebowitz, Joyce Rumery, Kim Schultz, and Virginia Witucke are all deserving of my gratitude. Justine Fiorello, Wanda Graham, Barbara Kirchner, Barbara McGuire, and Linda Neely have served the off-campus library program, the conference, and its proceedings with distinction. Judi Porter was unparalleled in her support. Without Judi's effort and her good humor the conferences and proceedings would have been considerably more cumbersome to initiate and complete.

A planning committee reflective of diverse academic and library programs as well as geographic locations facilitated each of the four conferences represented by the articles in this volume. The contribution of the planning committee members was most helpful to the success of the conferences and I am appreciative of their willingness to participate with us. I am particularly grateful to the librarians in England, Canada, and Australia who helped develop the Off-campus Library Services Conference into an international forum. Included among this latter group are Christine Crocker, Raymond Fisher, Alexander Slade, Craig Grimison and Yuen-Ching Sin Fu.

Finally, I wish to acknowledge the importance of the attendees and presenters of the Off-campus Library Services Conferences in St. Louis, Knoxville, Reno, and Charleston who encouraged the success of those meetings and a heightened interest in providing quality off-campus library services. My thanks to them all.

Introduction

This collection of articles is composed of five sections covering program and service models, off-campus library services and accreditation, faculty issues, aspects of off-campus library support in Australia, England, and Canada, and administrative issues. The papers included here were chosen to represent differing types of institutions and off-campus academic and library programs. These articles discuss aspects of off-campus library service from a variety of perspectives including that of the librarian, the accreditor, and the administrator.

John Weatherford's short paper on the Central Michigan University off-campus library program is a fitting one with which to begin this volume. Mr. Weatherford was largely responsible for the establishment of what is now one of the more highly sophisticated programs of its type. His article provides an outline of the early growth and development of the C.M.U. program. *Library Services for a Remote Campus* by Geneva Bush and James Damico is included as both an interesting service model and an excellent example of an agreement between non-affiliated institutions to provide off-campus library services. Dennis Lindberg and Eileen Chalfoun explain the creation of a program for off-campus library services throughout Vermont. H. Maynard Lowry's paper is useful for its description of a functional program and its insights to library services at international sites. The off-campus library program of St. Mary's College of California is discussed in detail by Stephanie Rogers Bangert. This program is illustrative of the kind of program which can be extended to off-campus learners regardless of the size of the parent academic institution.

Accreditation issues are covered in three articles beginning with an overview of regional standards by Antoinette Kania. Terrence MacTaggart discusses accreditation from the accreditor's perspective, while William Aguilar and Marie Kascus discuss the specific case of state licensure and accreditation in Connecticut.

Patricia Kelley's paper concerns a topic too little discussed, the impact on academic libraries by non-affiliated, off-campus students and faculty. John and Mary Lou Cook share the results of their studies to determine the interest in library services by off-campus faculty. Richard Potter discusses an innovative program designed to provide off-campus faculty with improved access to instructional materials. This latter program is indicative of the creativity to be found within the sphere of off-campus library services.

Three papers cover very different aspects of off-campus library services in Australia, England, and Canada. Christine Crocker, Raymond Fisher, and Alexander Slade have each been actively involved with the development and maturation of off-campus library services in their individual countries and these papers reflect facets of their commitment to this kind of service.

The contribution by Mary Joyce Pickett, Brian Nielsen, and Susan Swords Steffen describes an off-campus library support service which acts as a catalyst for continuing education programming. Here is an example of how a private research university responded to its off-campus environment. Branch libraries play a significant role away from the main academic campus and the paper by Barbara Kemp and Maureen Pastine describes branch library development from the administrative perspective. Anne Mathews discusses both the provision of quality off-campus library services and federal grants which may be applicable to those designing or enhancing such programs. Nancy Burich describes an organizational structure for off-campus library support.

The editor began an association with off-campus library services in August 1979 that continues to the present time. It has been an affiliation marked by learning, a broadening of horizons, and a recognition of the need for non-traditional adult education opportunities and the library services which can support them. It was clear early on that this was an area of library service with both affinities to and differences from on-campus academic library programs. The support of Central Michigan University's off-campus students and faculty encompassed aspects of both on-campus public and technical services. At the same time, it was also exceedingly and sometimes painfully clear that off-campus library services embraced challenges not generally found within the framework of the on-campus library experience. Further, this was not an area of library science which was discussed to any great extent in the library literature. A sense of professional isolation was an important motivating factor in the development and implementation of the Off-campus Library Services Conference.

Those of us at Central Michigan University lacked information about what other institutions were doing in support of their off-campus constituents. We wanted the answers to any number of questions that might help us complete our charge of library service. Which if any other institutions had programs which provided off-campus library support? What form did these programs take? How were other institutions responding to issues of licensure and accreditation in the off-campus environment? And most importantly, who were the librarians involved with off-campus library services? We acknowledged that networking had as great a potential here as in other areas of librarianship.

Given the support of Library Director John Weatherford and Provost John Cantelon and the financial backing of the University's Institute for Personal and Career Development, the Off-campus Library Services Conference was first convened in St. Louis, Missouri in 1982. Like many first time ventures, the risks of undertaking this endeavor were quite real.

The conference was successful and, with the three other conferences which quickly followed, allowed us to share experiences while providing a national, and then international, forum for discussion and creative involvement. Participation from a variety of practitioners representing all sizes of institutions and vastly differing academic and library programs aided the development of the conference and helped to sharpen its focus on the exchange of information relevant to the field.

As Central Michigan University prepares for its fifth conference in this series, it is most exciting to be witness to and participant in other activities concerning off-campus library services which may have been fostered by or made easier owing to the increased attention caused by this conference. The Association of College and Research Libraries (ACRL) issued revised Guidelines for Extended Campus Library Services in 1989 which update those issued originally in 1967 and revised in 1980. Hearings in regard to the latest revision were a part of the 1988 Charleston conference. Another important development concerning ACRL was that organization's creation of a section devoted to off-campus services. Although the Extended Campus Library Services Section is in its infancy, it is already furthering efforts to facilitate networking and the exchange of information about off-campus library activity. The ACRL Board of Directors, with its vote to establish the newest of its sections, has focused attention on this aspect of librarianship and allowed the association to play a greater role in the programming of this arena. There has also been an increase in publication about off-campus library services. Two works are of particular importance. *Library Services for Off-campus and Distance Education: An Annotated Bibliography* by Sheila Latham, Alexander L. Slade, and Carol Budnick was published earlier this year. This volume of joint Canadian, American, and British publication is already proving its value by improving access to the literature of international off-campus library support. In addition, the Spring 1991 issue of *Library Trends* is devoted to off-campus library services. With its articles covering diverse topics such as the ACRL Guidelines, accreditation, military bases, model programs, applications of technology, etc., this volume should prove useful to a variety of academicians with interests in adult and continuing education.

The articles in this volume are but a sampling of the many papers presented at Central Michigan University's Off-campus Library Services Conference. They are offered here to enhance the reader's knowledge and appreciation of the off-campus library support environment. A contributing factor in the creation the Off-campus Library Services Conference was a desire to improve awareness of this type of library support. These articles, many of which have been revised and/or augmented, are part of a continuing effort to reach that goal.

Barton M. Lessin

Prerequisites for Campus-quality Library Services to External Degree Programs[1]

John W. Weatherford

In such an assembly as this, where innovators are the rule, I must pick my way gingerly lest I tell you merely what you already know. Probably all I have to offer here is a managerial view of the Central Michigan University distant library service which was in my portfolio of cares and joys at its inception.

The library began this project with several assumptions, assumptions that experience gave us no reason to alter:

1. We would not attempt to set up little libraries wherever the external degree program operated, not even a central "extension" library on the Wisconsin or Florida model, but make the entire collection of the Central Michigan University library available, either by copying or by circulation.

2. Libraries at the distant sites would in general prove helpful but not wholly adequate for our purposes. We would cultivate rapport with them, but never become dependent on them.

3. Library service would be free of charge to extended degree students--even such elements as copying for which we charge on-campus clients.

4. The external degree administration would best know its general library needs, for example, whether it wished to have library service in North Dakota; and the library administration would best know what constitutes adequate library service and how to provide it.

5. Students and faculty at distant sites would be encouraged to deal directly with the home library as they would if they were on-campus, without going through any other channels.

6. The service could succeed only if aggressively sold to students and faculty, and only librarians could do this.

7. The main use of library materials would be for independent paper-writing rather than assigned readings.

8. Financial support would be provided by exploiting large assets by relatively small incremental expenditures. By assets, I mean the resources already owned by the university and open to distant library service.

Assets would include for example a building, and administrative support such as accounting services and time spent on planning and decision-making by administrators with broad responsibilities. By far the greatest of these assets is the library collection. Even dedicated collections range in R.K. Fisher's study (1978) up to 122,000 volumes for collections dedicated to distant service in the United States and up to 175,000 volumes in the United Kingdom. Dedicated collections of this kind are not what I mean by assets because they would be an incremental expense of the distant service. I am speaking of an entire university collection made available for distant service. For convenience, let us refer to it as the home collection. For the home collection to be an asset in distant service, it must be strong of course in distant areas of study. The Central Michigan University library's home collection managed to provide 75% of the books and periodicals requested by its distant master's degree students, who especially in the early years made their requests without usually knowing whether the home collection can meet them or not. (This experience, incidentally offers better opportunities to assess the adequacy of the collection than our home experience, where often clients request only those books and periodicals that they think we have.)

We have some clue to the value of freeing our entire collection for distant service. In a sample of two months' requests to the home library from clients scattered among our distant service sites in April and August of 1982, 64% of the requests satisfied by books and periodicals lay in the Library of Congress classifications of the H's, 9% in government documents, and 27% in the LC classes remaining, except for the C's, M's, and S's, which alone had not been called for in the sample months. If we had set up a separate, dedicated collection comprising only the H's, our ability to fill requests would have had only 64% of the collection that we actually drew on.

To be an asset, anybody's home collection must be not only strong but retrievable. As you know, retrievability at a distance varies enormously according to the discipline involved. I need not tell you that *The Astonished Muse* and *The Well-Wrought Urn* are less revealing titles than "Paleogenesis and Paleopidemiology of Primate Malaria" or even

Insania Pingens. Luck has been with us, giving us only external degree programs in which our home collection is strong, and comprising only the more retrievable subjects. What if a distant learning program required materials on a large scale in which the home collection is weak, or at the wrong end of the retrievability spectrum? These would be limits on the assets available for distant services.

Even if we did not encounter these limits at Central Michigan University, they are substantial. They are waiting for you and me, and within present technology they may prove insuperable if we do encounter them. I suggest that the best solution of this difficulty is already embodied in R.K. Fisher's seventh recommendation for the United States: "No extension course should be approved or accredited without previous evidence of adequate library support ..." (Fisher, p. 72).

Distant library service depends not only on these assets but on their effective delivery. Delivery in our model is an incremental cost of distant delivery service and it constitutes the bulk of the distant library service budget. Typically this budget has included: librarians and support staff employed exclusively in this program, support staff relieving temporary congestion created by the program in processing at the home library, book and periodical purchases to strengthen the program, as well as travel, telephone, OCLC, postage, and photocopy.

Now let us see what leverage we created. For eighty-six dollars per full-time student in 1982 the external degree program obtained library service. Compare this with the home cost of $150 per full-time student, where retrievability is easier and delivery a negligible problem. The incremental funding by the external administration has thus opened to it assets far exceeding its capacity to purchase.

The external degree program, because it produces net income, can in turn support the more familiar off-campus program, the kind that provides standard courses, stays in one state, receives partial subsidy from that state, charges its students only the normal tuition for regular on campus courses, and could never pay for the kind of library service enjoyed by its more affluent sister, the external degree program. The orthodox off-campus program can, however, afford the incremental cost of building a similar library service on the distant library structure, funded as just described.

This is enough so far, I hope, to show that the current income of a revenue-producing external degree operation can combine with already available assets of the parent university library to provide an aggressive and persuasive library service, and a little serendipity for the more traditional off-campus program as well. How effectively this income and these assets combine depends on their organizational relationship.

From the literature you have probably noticed some variety of organizational structures. In ours, there were two principal parties: the library (which has the assets) and the external degree administration (which has the incremental funds and the need for the service). The formal organ for bringing the two parties together was a joint steering committee comprising representatives of each: usually the director and assistant to the director for the library and the director and ad hoc participants (such as academic or business officer) for the external degree administration.

The two parties were equal in the steering committee. Impasse was to be resolved by the provost of the university, to whom both directors reported. As a practical matter, there was no such impasse after the first two years or so. The chief but not the only product of this committee was the budget.

The budget was administered by the assistant to the director of libraries as budget director for the external degree library program. The budget did not have rigid line items beyond agreed distinctions among salaries, wages, equipment, and other types of expenditure, although care was taken to keep expenditures to the spirit of the agreement made in the steering committee. In any operation as fluid as this, the annual budget often undergoes interim revisions to accommodate, say, a new geographical area. These revisions were made in the same manner as the budget.

I believe this is still the structure of our particular distant library service: 1) the entire university library collection available; 2) delivery at costs to the external degree program proportionally less than those familiar to on-campus administrations; and 3) an organization that recognizes both the paramount needs of the client and the expertise in the library.

Reference

Fisher, R.K. (1978). Library Services to University Extension Students in the U.S.A., A Critical Survey, with Comparative Assessment of Equivalent Services in Great Britain. *The British Library Research and Development Reports*, no. 5432.

Note

[1] Mr. Weatherford's paper was presented at the first Off-campus Library Services Conference, St. Louis, Missouri, and appeared in the 1983 edition of the conference proceedings.

Library Services for a Remote Campus[1]

Geneva L. Bush and James A. Damico

Introduction

The University of South Alabama (USA) is located in the city of Mobile on the Gulf Coast. It is the only major public institution of higher learning within a fifty mile radius of the city, serving not only Mobile, Alabama, but also the Mississippi and Florida coast areas. With an enrollment of over ten thousand students the University offers fifty-seven bachelors, twenty-three masters, and seven doctoral programs. The University of South Alabama-Baldwin County (USABC) was established in 1984 to meet the upper-division, higher education needs in one of the fastest growing counties in Alabama. Classes are held in Fairhope with library services offered at the Fairhope Public Library, and in Bay Minette at Faulkner State Junior College Library providing services to USABC students. The distance from Mobile to Fairhope is thirty-four miles, from Fairhope to Bay Minette is twenty-nine miles and from Bay Minette to Mobile is thirty-one miles.

Administration

The University Branch is under Academic Affairs. The Dean of Continuing Education, who reports to the Vice President for Academic Affairs, has overall responsibility for the University Branch. The Director of the branch reports directly to the Dean. The Head of Library Branch Operations reports to both the Director of University Libraries and the Director of the University Branch. The Librarian, in reporting to the University Librarian, is a member of the Libraries Administrative Council, and coordinates library support for course planning, notifies faculty teaching at the branch to determine information needs of students, and coordinates services at the branch libraries.

The specific duties of the Head of Library Branch Operations include maintenance of library services for faculty and students, providing public services to students at remote sites, and providing use of electronic technology for access to reference services and library collections at the main campus. This position requires extensive travel to provide the materials needed by faculty and students.

Programs

Upper level undergraduate and graduate courses at the Baldwin County campus are concentrated in the disciplines of Arts and Sciences, Business and Management Studies, Education, and Nursing. More specifically, the courses offered by Arts and Sciences include biology, communications, English literature, geology, political science, psychology and sociology. The Business program includes courses in money and banking, and marketing. In Education, courses include Growth and Development, the Young Child, Exceptional Children and Youth, Teaching and Learning Evaluation, and Leisure Services. Currently, about 35 courses per quarter are being offered. Non-credit programs are offered to the Baldwin County community as well.

Faculty and Students

The Baldwin County Campus uses faculty from the main campus for all educational programs stressing a commitment to provide the same high-quality educational programs currently being offered on the main campus. In 1986-87, enrollment by college was as follows:

	Number	%
Arts & Science	276	20
Business & Management Studies	99	7
Education	530	39
Nursing	228	17
Special Programs	188	14
Other	39	2

A profile of the student population indicates that 65% are over the age of 25. Most are enrolled in evening courses, and almost half are part-time. During the Fall quarter 1986 there were approximately 121 full-time and 213 part-time students for a total enrollment of 334. The initial enrollment figures for fall quarter of 1987 show an increase of 8.2%, or 365 students.

Types of Information

Information requests (1986-1987) from the USABC community were divided into requests for specific items and requests for information on specified subjects. The total requests for this academic year are divided as follows: books, 66.5%; journal articles, 34.9%; and computer-assisted literature searches, 7.6%. The majority of the requests in each area are from the field of education.

Book Requests by LC Classification Number:

	%		%
B	8.3	L	24.4
E	3.3	N	2.3
F	1.0	P	19.7
G	3.6	Q	2.0
H	9.3	R(W)	10.7
J	6.0	S	.3
K	3.3	T	2.6

Journal Requests by Academic Area of Requestor:

	%
Education	65.3
Non-USA	16.0
Sociology	11.3
Nursing	6.6

Computer Assisted Literature Searches by Database:

	%
ERIC	37.8
INFO	10.8
PSYC	8.1

MESH	5.4
TOUR	5.4

AARP, A400, ACHI, BBIP, GPOM, HAZE, NOOZ, NTIS, OCLC, PTSP, SFDB all used less than 1% each.

Document Delivery

When the planning for library and information services for USABC was done in early 1985, procedures for handling document delivery by mail and courier service were approved by the Public Services Committee of the University Libraries. The requests for specific items were to be filled by the Interlibrary Loan Department of the University Library with assistance from the Interlibrary Loan Department of the Biomedical Library for medically related requests. As the program developed, the USABC Librarian, making weekly trips to the main campus to attend committee meetings and to fill requests for unspecified material on given subjects, filled the item specific requests personally. All requests are processed on a weekly basis unless an emergency situation arises. Requests forms for main campus materials are available in both the Fairhope Public Library (FPL) and the Faulkner State Junior College Library (FSJC).

Items received from the campus libraries are taken to either FSJC or FPL, depending on where the request originated. Books are then checked out to the requestor and photocopy fees are collected by the circulation staff of the library. The books can be renewed at the library where it is picked up. Books checked out from the main campus library by a student remain that student's responsibility until returned to the main campus. Returning these books to the USABC Librarian, FSJC, or FPL does not constitute returning the book "on time." The USABC Librarian will return books checked out by a student, but any overdue fines incurred are still charged to the student. The Librarian makes every effort to ensure that the books reach the campus library before becoming overdue and will take the overdue fine from the student to the USA Library with the material if the need arises. See Appendix A for text of the official USA Libraries policy on USABC circulation.

Marketing of Services

A brochure describing library and information services for students in Baldwin County classes is distributed in each class during the first two weeks of the quarter. In each class services available are described and how, when, and where to contact the USABC Librarian is explained. Brochures are also distributed at registration and placed in USABC offices and Baldwin County libraries. Appendix B includes the informational text from this brochure.

Each quarter a short notice is placed in the FSJC student newsletter regarding the availability of materials from USA Libraries. On two occasions articles written by USA's Public Relations Department were printed in the Baldwin County newspapers.

The USABC Librarian keeps lines of communication open to the public libraries of the county, meeting with the librarians as a group and individually to explain library services available through USABC. Informed, they will be able to refer any of our students who might approach them regarding library services.

Faculty scheduled to teach in the USABC program are contacted prior to the beginning of the quarter in order to ensure the awareness of library services. Help is offered with reserve materials, audio-visual set-up, and library related assignments. The Librarian's schedule for the quarter is given to each faculty member to facilitate contact.

Interlibrary Cooperation

A librarian was added to the staff of USABC at the request of FSJC. An agreement with another institution prior to USA's involvement with Baldwin County head at one time supplied a librarian to the FSJC campus. Because FSJC has only one full-time librarian on their campus in Bay Minette and a part-time librarian on their branch campus in Fairhope, there was need for another academic librarian in the county, especially with the introduction of USA students into the county. The stipulation for a librarian was in the original contract between the two institutions. The two institutions did not sign the contract, but the commitment to a librarian for the branch program was maintained.

In October, 1986, a formal agreement was written and signed by USABC, FPL, and USA Libraries. This agreement put into writing the cooperation that had been building since the beginning of the USABC program. What follows is the text of the 1987-88 agreement. It is modeled on one written by St. Joseph's College (Travis, 1982).

Cooperative Agreement

The University of South Alabama-Baldwin County and the Fairhope Public Library have goals that can be addressed by a cooperative arrangement between the two institutions. Both are interested in offering the best library services possible to their patrons.

This agreement is not a finite list of rights and responsibilities for either institution, but defines the spirit of cooperation previously observed.

1.   The University will instruct its Baldwin County students in the procedures and regulations in force at the Fairhope Public Library as well as the specifics of this agreement.

2.   Reference services will be available to University of south Alabama-Baldwin County students in the Fairhope Public Library.

3.   Students who are not eligible for Fairhope Public Library cards will have borrowing privilege normally extended to holders of Fairhope Library cards upon presentation of a valid University of South Alabama identification card.

4.   University of South Alabama-Baldwin County students will be expected to abide by all the rules and regulations of the Fairhope Public Library.

5.   The University of South Alabama-Baldwin County will assume responsibility for the cost of materials damaged or not returned after a reasonable length of time. This refers to items checked out using a University of South Alabama identification card.

6.   The University of South Alabama-Baldwin County may place items on reserve in the Fairhope Public Library, striving to have loan periods compatible with Fairhope Public Library circulation policies.

7.   Any items purchased by the University and placed in the Fairhope Public Library remain the property of the University.

8.   The Fairhope Public Library Director may request items from the University of South Alabama Libraries through the Head of Library Branch Operations or interlibrary loan.

9.   The Fairhope Public Library may expect the Head of Library Branch Operations for the University to be in the Fairhope Public Library two nights a week during the University's quarter. The schedule is determined by the schedule of University of South Alabama-Baldwin county classes for a given quarter.

10.   Fairhope Public Library patrons may request computer assisted literature searches, and receive the service on a cost recovery basis. (This is the same service offered to University of south Alabama-Baldwin County students.)

11.   The University of South Alabama-Baldwin County will pay to Fairhope Public Library an annual fee based on the number of quarter hours generated in Fairhope during the immediately preceding four quarter period. For the period October 19XX through September 19XX, the fee will be $___.

12.   The University of South Alabama-Baldwin County will pay to Fairhope Public Library an annual fee of $___, in addition to the above, for janitorial services rendered for the adjacent classroom space and facilities.

An agreement was already in place between FSJC and FPL. Their contract provided for reciprocal borrowing, FSJC materials to be placed at FPL, one professional and one assistant to work part-time during the evenings, and a subsidy for staying open longer hours.

All there institutions work together to provide the best available library services to all patrons in the area. USABC's advent helped in the area of staffing as well as providing direct access to the academic collections of the USA Libraries. The following are areas of service provided on a cooperative basis.

1.   Circulation - FSJC and USABC students are allowed to check out items from FPL upon presentation of valid student identification cards.

FPL patrons are allowed to request items from the College and University collections through their Librarians, who first ascertain the legitimacy of the request. USABC students are also allowed to check out materials from FSJC using their USA student identification cards. Circulation periods, overdue fines, etc., are based on the lending library, nor the student affiliation. Eight percent of the total items retrieved from the USA Libraries were for FSJC or FPL patrons.

2.   Audio-Visual Equipment - This is a shared services, each institution making available pieces not owned by the others and taking care of everyday activities such as changing bulbs and scheduling use of equipment.

3.   Reference - There is cooperation in at least three functions: reference desk service, computer assisted literature searching, and bibliographic instruction. All librarians provide the same level of service to anyone asking a reference question. Affiliation is only considered if the question cannot be answered and the patron or query needs to be referred.

4.   Computer Assisted Literature Searching - Provided through the USABC librarian. Neither of the other institutions have searching facilities at this time. Thirteen and one-half percent of the searches done by the USABC Librarian were for non-USA patrons. These searches are billed as if the person requesting the search were a student of USA. No service fees are added as they would be on campus for non-USA requestors.

5.   Bibliographic Instruction - Sessions are presented by the USABC Librarian for any group or class scheduled to meet during evening hours on duty at either FSJC or FPL. Therefore, the USABC Librarian conducts library usage instruction for USABC and FSJC classes during the evening hours. Sessions are presented to English, literature, history, sociology, psychology, criminal justice, education and adult personalized studies classes. Sessions are held in the library chosen by the faculty member requesting the instruction.

Evaluation and Recommendations

During 1986-87, two reports were received by the Baldwin County campus. One was a consultant's report, the other from the Southern Association of Colleges and Schools Visiting Committee. The following statement is taken from the consultant's report concerning library services.

> The current library situation seems to be working well. It is questionable whether it would continue to be functional if the student population and course offerings increase. There is a need for the development of a basic library at Fairhope which would be independent of the public library and the junior college library. The furnishings of adequate library resources necessary to the kind of extensive programs which appear to be planned would quickly swamp the resources now available. The current staff apparently meets the demands of the current enrollment. However, here again, adequate planning would lead to a rational and orderly expansion of staff to support the needs of the students in the area.

The Southern Association's report made suggestions after their representatives' site visit in August 1986. Under Section IV: Educational Programs - Curriculum and Instruction, they noted:

> A problem mentioned by students in the area of library support service was that the library closes at the Bay Minette campus on Friday afternoon and does not reopen until Monday morning. Students expressed the concern that they had more time to spend in the library on weekends than at any other time. Students also expressed the concern that they had more time to spend in the library on weekends than at any other time. Students also expressed concern that they often had to return books to the main campus, and considered this an inconvenience and hindrance to library usage. The Committee suggests that the library schedule be reviewed to determine student time-use effectiveness.

Additionally in Section V: Education Support Services - Library and Learning Resources, they state:

> The Baldwin County Branch of the University of South Alabama is staffed with a well-qualified, full-time, professional academic librarian who is responsible for all library services provided by the University in Baldwin

County. In some cases the librarian will personally check out books from the main campus library as a service to students enrolled at the Baldwin Campus. The Committee feels that this is a commendable effort to ensure access to library resources but suggests that the practice be monitored very carefully.

The concerns mentioned in the above statements are ones we are cognizant of in the library and in the University Administration. The University Library monitors the increase-decrease in service on a quarter-by-quarter basis.

The Future

As mentioned in the introduction, Baldwin County is one the fastest growing counties in the state of Alabama. The University of South Alabama branch campus will undoubtedly expand as more demands for higher education are made by residents of the county. Library services will grow proportionately and must eventually have a permanent collection and staff. One event that has happened sooner that expected is dial access capability to the library's LUIS (Library User Information System) online catalog. Not only will the Branch Librarian and students have access to the University Libraries' holdings from Fairhope, but from Bay Minette as well. Plans to expand the facilities located in Fairhope are in place and, as stated earlier, the library will continue to monitor library use and needs and expand services where needed. We are excited that the University and Library continue to play a vital role in higher education in Baldwin County.

Addendum

Since 1987, the Baldwin county Branch of the University of South Alabama has made several major changes in response to the needs of its student population and the relocation of an academic division. While some classes are still held in Bay Minette, the main Baldwin County office and the majority of classes are now located in Fairhope. Fairhope is more centrally located in the county and is the hub of the population concentration and growth. In 1988, a Mobile County hospital was purchased to house USA's Nursing Division. Since this location is relatively close to the Baldwin County campus, the decision was made to discontinue the branch's nursing courses. Even with the loss of this program, the growth of the branch campus has been tremendous as evident by the average credit hour enrollment figures below:

	1986/87	1989/90
Arts and Sciences	501	880
Business and Management	156	442
Education	652	1147
Nursing	306	0
Special Programs	120	70

The total enrollment has increased 39% from 334 in 1987 to 463 in 1990.

The library services have kept pace with the enrollment growth through the addition of several computerized services and a part-time clerk. Dial access to the main library's on-line catalog (LUIS) was added in 1988. In early 1990, the InfoTrac database and the SIGI career guidance program were added to the branch services. The hardware and program for ERIC is on order and should be in place by Summer, 1990. Development of a core collection is underway, but as with most new branches, additional facilities are needed for library services, a computer lab and additional classrooms. Since these needs are directly related to the growth of the branch, the staff views them as a good "problem" to have.

Reference

Travis, T.G., Watson, S.D., Martin, P.W., & Roberts, C. (1982). Library service for noncampus students. *College & Research Libraries News*, *43*, 88.

Note

[1] The paper prepared by Geneva L. Bush and James A. Damico was presented at the fourth Off-campus Library Services Conference, Charleston, South Carolina, and appeared in the 1989 edition of the conference proceedings.

Appendix A

University of South Alabama Libraries
Library Branch Operations

Pertains to: Library services in Baldwin County (USABC)

1.0 USABC Circulation
   1.1   Circulation of USA Libraries' materials. (Except IMC materials. See 1.3)
      Materials will be requested by the USABC Librarian and charged out to USABC. Materials will then be charged to the requesting patron through the circulation desk of either the Faulkner State Junior College Library (FSJC) or the Fairhope Public Library (FPL).
   1.1.1 Patrons
      USABC for:
      A.   Students with valid USA identification cards.
      B.   Students with valid FSJC identification cards.
      Note: These students may not check out materials directly from the USA Libraries.
   1.1.2 Loan periods
      A.   At FSJC: Two weeks, not to extend beyond the last day of classes for the current USA academic term.
      B.   At FPL: Three weeks, not to extend beyond the last day of classes for the current USA academic term.
      C.   Reserve materials (both locations): Set by professor and the USABC librarian.
   1.1.3 Fines and penalties
      A.   Overdue fines: Assessed by FSJC or FPL circulation desk, based on their respective fine schedules.
      B.   Replacement costs and rebinding fees: Assessed by the USA Libraries through the USABC librarian.
      C.   Blocks

1. During an academic term:
    Students may be blocked from borrowing further materials for any of the following reasons.
    a. Overdue items.
    b. Fines
    c. Unpaid charges for lost or damaged materials.
    d. Failure to return items that have been recalled within three days after recall.
    e. Checks returned for "Insufficient funds".
2. At the end of the USA academic term:
    Students who have not returned all materials and/or paid all fines, replacement costs or rebinding fees will have blocks placed against them with the appropriate Office of the Registrar. These blocks will prevent them from registering for subsequent academic terms or obtaining transcripts from the Registrar until all materials have been returned and/or all financial obligations are discharged.
    a. USA students are reported and cleared by the USABC librarian through the USA libraries' circulation department.
    b. FSJC students are reported and cleared by the FSJC librarian.

1.2 Circulation of FSJC and FPL materials to USABC students
1.2.1 Patrons: USABC students with valid USA identification cards.
1.2.2 Loan periods: See 1.1.2 A and C above.
1.2.3 Fines and penalties
   A. Overdue fines: See 1.1.3 above.
   B. Replacement costs and rebinding fees: Assessed by the lending librarian.
   C. Blocks: See 1.1.3 C above.
1.3 Circulation of IMC materials and equipment.
1.3.1 Patrons: USABC faculty
1.3.2 Requests
   A. For classroom use only.
   B. USABC faculty may make requests through the USABC librarian or directly to the IMC. If requests responsible for the pick-up and return of the material and/or equipment.

1.3.3 General Information
>   All policies of the IMC, as stated in the USA Libraries'
>   Circulation Policy, will be followed.

Submitted by: Geneva Bush
Date: December 13, 1985
Approved by: University Libraries' Faculty
Date: December 13, 1985
Promulgation date: Immediately

Appendix B

Baldwin County Library and Information Services

USA Library Branch Operations
The University of South Alabama Libraries

We at the University of South Alabama Baldwin County (USABC) and
the USA Libraries want to insure your success as a university student
by providing you with the best most relevant library and information
services available. The library and Information services available to
students enrolled in our classes are described briefly in this brochure.
for more information on any or all of these services, please contact the
USABC librarian at the phone number and/or address given on the
back of this brochure. We welcome suggestions for improvement of
these services or for addition of new services which are needed.

LOCAL PARTICIPATING LIBRARIES:

Learning Resources Center
Faulkner State Junior college
Bay Minette, Alabama 36507
Director: Barbara Moseley
Telephone: ( )

Fairhope Public Library
161 North Section Street
Fairhope, Alabama 36530
Director: Betty Suddeth
Telephone: ( )

As of this printing there are two local participating libraries. Call the
USABC librarian to see if any others have been added to the program.

ACCESS TO USA LIBRARIES:

On the Mobile campus, students may use their USA student
identification cards to access materials in the USA Libraries. ID cards
are Issued quarterly for both full-time and part-time USABC students.

For more information on orientation to the USA Libraries, see the section LIBRARY INSTRUCTION AND ORIENTATION.

ACCESS TO LOCAL PARTICIPATING LIBRARIES:

USABC students may use their USA student identification cards to borrow materials in local participating libraries. ID cards are issued quarterly for both full-time and part-time USABC students. Loan periods and overdue lines are defined by the local participating library, not the USA Libraries.

LIBRARY INSTRUCTION AND ORIENTATION:

Instruction in how to access and use relevant library resources is important academic success. In fact, acquiring good information skills is a necessary part of the lifelong learning process. To refresh and refurbish library and information-finding skills, orientation and instruction in library use is available to USABC students at USABC campus locations as well as on the Mobile campus.

In coordination with faculty, the USABC librarian will meet with classes at USABC campus sites to discuss library services and to review resources available in local participating libraries and the USA Libraries. On the Mobile campus, individuals and/or groups may schedule an appointment with USABC librarian to explore the resources of the USA Libraries. In consideration of the USABC student, scheduling is flexible and can include nights and weekends.

RESERVE MATERIALS:

The USABC Librarian will assist faculty in obtaining and organizing reserve materials use in USABC classes. These materials may include books, journal articles, government documents and reference works. Every effort is made to see that these materials are easily available for student use. Reserves are placed in the most convenient and accessible local participating library.

Development of Off-campus Library Services in the Vermont State Colleges[1]

Dennis Lindberg and Eileen Chalfoun

Developing library services for off-campus students in the Vermont State Colleges has been conceived as an integral part of the development of library services generally in the system. Concern for services not on campuses has led to choices which emphasize technology, coordination, and cooperation between existing college libraries. This paper examines the planning process and its results first in the system as a whole, and then in the Community College of Vermont, an non-campus, non-traditional college without a library.

Background

The Vermont State Colleges (VSC) is a public corporation which includes three four-year institutions with small graduate programs in education (Castleton, Johnson and Lyndon State Colleges), a two-year technical college (Vermont Technical College-VTC), and the Community College of Vermont (CCV). Total head count is about 7,500 amounting to about 5,000 F.T.E. (Full-Time Equivalents).

The Community College operates state-wide from twelve site offices and does not have campuses of full-time faculty. With about 2,500 it is the largest in head count, but the smallest in F.T.E. (about 750). The four campus-based colleges also operate off-campus programs, involving in several cases significant numbers of students. The four campus colleges have libraries that provide services on campus. The community college does not have a library or librarians working as librarians.

Though blessed with a romantic image, one reality of Vermont is that it is a small, rural and relatively poor state. State support for the State Colleges is the lowest in the nation while tuition levels are the highest in the nation for such colleges. VSC receives a one-line appropriation from the legislature which in recent years accounts for about twenty-eight percent of total revenues. The balance is from student charges and Federal grants.

The system experienced a major financial crisis in the late 1970's as reality intruded upon the dreams of the 1960's and early 1970's. New, tough-minded managers were brought in to get the system back on its feet. After the roofs were fixed, the life-safety problems corrected, under-enrolled degree programs pruned, damage to accreditation statuses controlled and corrected, common financial and personnel systems put in place, and adequate, if unsophisticated, administrative computer systems installed, it was time, in 1982, to deal with the "library problem" and begin the process of improving academic quality generally.

With the fires out, the late Chancellor Richard E. Bjork gave one person (Lindberg) system-wide responsibility for computing, library development, and institutional research. He saw that the library problem was large, that it would take time to correct, and that investment in information technology might reduce the need for additional fixed assets like books and buildings for their storage.

Planning Process

To produce real results, planning cannot take place in a vacuum. It is not enough to figure out what ought to be done. In Vermont at least, a plan of action, and the assumptions underlying it, need to be perceived as reasonable, rational, practical and soundly conceived. The realities of the structure, politics and personalities of the organization are a factor in planning, as are the realities of the relationships between the organization and the external environment.

The Library Assessment Group

For these reasons and because other issues were at center stage in the fall of 1982, the library project began quietly. A system-wide Library Assessment Group (with the unfortunate acronym LAG) was assembled by the Chancellor to conduct a detailed assessment of VSC library and information services. Members were the four librarians from the campus colleges, an associate academic dean from one college who has an M.L.S., the director of CCV's Northern Region who chaired the college's Resource Committee, a staff member from CCV (Chalfoun), also an M.L.S. but not working as a librarian, and Lindberg, as chair and staff.

The assessment took nearly a year. Librarians reported in detail their judgements of the quality, quantity, adequacy, appropriateness, currentness, and rate of use of the collection supporting each degree program and the college's general education program. Reference and bibliographic instruction programs, automation and technical processing, staffing, and facilities were also described.

Two peer groups were developed, one of about twenty-five smaller, public, four-year institutions (all members of the American Association of State Colleges and Universities) and another of about twelve smaller, state-supported, two-year technical colleges. No non-campus community colleges with predominately classroom-based, coursework instruction could be found. CCV appeared to be unique and truly without peers. A two-page questionnaire was developed asking about enrollment, number of degree programs offered, reference and bibliographic instruction staffing and services, automation and technical processing, and facilities. Librarians were also asked to attach the most recent HEGIS survey with its data on holdings, staffing and expenditures.

In July 1982, the Group produced a thirty-eight page report for the Priorities (Executive) Committee of the Board of Trustees. Copies were distributed to all trustees and senior VSC administrators. The report was low-key and measured in tone, but candid and frank. It confirmed in detail what many knew to be generally true. Several presidents were concerned that the report not get into the press and affect recruiting.

The report concluded that collections are generally small, have significant gaps, are of uneven quality, often inappropriate, and not particularly current. Students come to VSC institutions knowing little about the use of libraries and there are few requirements built into the curriculum for students to use libraries. Bibliographic instruction is rudimentary and professional reference services are minimal at three of the four libraries. There is some use of on-line searching in the libraries, but no other significant use of information technology. Technical processing is not automated. Virtually no library services are provided to non-campus and off-campus students who make up about one-third of the system's students on a head count basis.

VSC institutions are weak when compared to ACRL standards. The four year institutions are also weak when compared to their peers. VTC looks strong in comparison to the other technical colleges, but only because, as a group, their libraries are so poor. Applying standards, CCV ought to have 95,000 volumes and three professionals in its library. Instead, it has claimed to rely on local public libraries, which in Vermont vary widely in size and quality, are generally unsuitable for supporting college level work, and are open an average of seventeen hours per week. While awarding CCV the maximum ten year renewal of its accreditation, it is not surprising that the New England Association had library support first on its list of problems to be addressed by the college before the next visit.

The informal work of the Assessment Group was perhaps as important as the formal work. Analysis of problems often leads to preliminary consideration of solutions, formally and informally, in and out of meetings. By the end of the process, there was general agreement that solutions would have to be system-wide solutions that serve CCV's non-campus students and the off-campus students of other colleges as well as those on campus. The group also began to think of the libraries as a single, though decentralized resource--four branches, but no main library.

Progress reports were regularly made to the Council of Presidents and the Council of Chief Academic Officers during the Assessment Groups' work. While little action resulted, a sense that "we're going to have to do something about the libraries" began to develop.

As the assessment process proceeded, VSC became an informal participant in a planning process under way among the University of Vermont, Middlebury College and the Vermont Department of Libraries to develop a joint distributed network including on-line catalogs and circulation and serials subsystems. VSC librarians participated in several of the technical subcommittees. A joint VSC system is expected to be one node in the network.

The assessment report was received by the Priorities Committee of the Board. It was mentioned, but not discussed in meetings of the full Board. Those Board members who read it were convinced by the weight of the evidence that the problem was large and must be address.

The Task Force on Library Development

The next step was for the Chancellor to appoint a system-wide Task

Force on Library Development in the Fall of 1983, again related to the Priorities Committee. To underscore the importance of the task, the presidents of the five colleges were appointed. Two of the librarians, two faculty members, an academic dean, a business manager, a CCV regional director, a CCV staff member (Chalfoun), a library staff member and a student were the other members. Members represented themselves, their college and their function. The Task Force was chaired by Lindberg who also served as the task Force's staff support.

The Task Force met six times during the year, weighing courses of action in dealing with reference services and bibliographic instruction, automation, and collection development and maintenance as well as the realities of VSC funding. Consensus developed with time. The range of points of view represented and the individual credibility of the participants at their college and within their system-wide functional groups (deans, business managers, etc.) gave the process general credibility throughout the system.

The Priorities Committee received all the Task Force materials, including background readings. Written and verbal progress reports were made at monthly meetings of the full board. The chairman of the board was particularly interested and began early to prepare the Board for what he knew would come. "Listen up folks," he said at one meeting. "Fixing this problem is going to cost real money."

In August 1984 the Task Force's recommendations were submitted to the board. Major points were:

1. appropriate information competencies in general education and degree programs;

2. parity between on-campus and off-campus programs in requirements for and use of library/information resources;

3. a single, joint on-line catalog as one node in a network also including the University of Vermont, Middlebury College and the State Department of Libraries. OCLC will be implemented and retrospective conversion performed on existing collections. The system will be accessible for off-campus and non-campus students and faculty through dial-up lines and will have full Boolean capabilities;

4. increased reference services including reference librarians for the

Community College of Vermont (CCV). CCV will have responsibility for reference services for off-campus students system-wide and will have incoming WATS lines;

5. a joint serials list, increased use of on-line searching especially at CCV, and digital facsimile transverse for the four libraries and the three CCV regional offices;

6. a five-year coordinated collection catch-up program to add 15,000 volumes per year to system holdings, including small reference collections for CCV site offices; and,

7. increased funding for collection renewal to reduce the book replacement cycle from 32.3 years at present to 20 years at the four-year colleges and 12 years at the technical colleges

Costs are projected to be $2.6 million in one-time (capital) funds and increments to the annual operating budget totaling $561,000. The report was received by the Board and endorsed in principle.

The decision to combine the catalogs in a single on-line system is particular important for non-campus and off-campus students and faculty as there will be one point of access for all VSC holdings and electronic mail capability within the system for ordering materials.

Implementation

Implementation is under way. Tasks have been divided into three categories: those requiring little or no funds, those covered in the fiscal year 1985 budget, and those requiring additional funding-- including fiscal year 1986 tasks needing $766,000 for full funding. Non-economic tasks include academic policy issues and cooperation between libraries to develop the joint serials list (done), target collection development efforts (in process) and developing a common policy for on-line searches (in process). Budgeted funds exist in fiscal year 1985 to implement OCLC, contract for retroconversion, and install digital facsimile machines. The former has begun.

State appropriations have been requested for the full amount of the project. Initial signs are mixed. The need is understood and accepted by the Governor-elect. She is, however, working to eliminate a budget deficit left by her predecessor. Revenue collections through March will affect success. Prospects for support in fiscal year 1987 are much better. Fund raising from private sources is also underway and tuition increases may also be sought.

While full implementation of the recommendations is down the road, the planning process has also stirred the pot in each of the colleges. The Community College of Vermont, particularly, because of its accreditation report and the system-wide process has begun to rethink its approach to delivering library and information services to its students.

Community College of Vermont

How to provide library services to the Community College of Vermont was one of the principle questions driving the VSC library development project. Founded in 1970 as a non-campus college, CCV has always seen itself as in the vanguard of higher education. It has received national recognition as one of the most creative, innovative, nontraditional institutions in the country.

One of the basic assumptions underlying the structure of this new institution was that many of the educational needs of the citizenry, particularly the rural and disadvantage, could be met through the utilization and coordination of existing resources. No new buildings were to be constructed, no library to be purchased, and no cafeteria services provided. Resources within local communities were to be used to accomplish the college's mission. Thus, flexibility became its greatest strength.

The problem which has constantly faced CCV is how to secure the educational resources to provide equal opportunity throughout the state to all of the students. Given a limited budget and minimal staffing, how can the college provide students the opportunity to fulfill its goals: a variety of choices, use of community resources, individually designed programs, transferability to other institutions, vocational guidance, recognition of experiential learning, staff development, alternative educational programs, regular evaluation, developmental programs and student support services. The list is replete with expensive items demanding careful and creative attention.

In order to explore creative answers to the college's problems, the structure of the institution must be understood. CCV site offices stretch from the Canadian border in the north to the Massachusetts state line in the south, and hug the border New Hampshire and New York on either side. Newport, St. Albans, Brattleboro, Bennington and White River Junction are the visible markers that outline the college's boundaries within the state. Within the state are many other site offices which maintain communication with the central administration in Waterbury.

Few site offices are within comfortable reach of research facilities and the college maintains no permanent library collections. In truth the public library system is the college's library system. With branches in virtually every Vermont community, students, in theory, have access through interlibrary loan to one million titles in the state including those held in the twenty-two college and university libraries. But sharing the woes of Tantalus, a student has little means of identifying relevant materials and usually finds the interlibrary loan process slow if not painful. Students throughout the state do not have equal access to the resources needed to do college-level research. Those writing a term paper may indeed have to wait a term in order to do a bibliographic search and access materials.

The college has attempted to develop a college-wide resource system to help instructors and students identify and locate print, audiovisual, and human resources identified in college records. Distance and poor communication facilities have prevented that system from ever being used effectively. By the time information was collected, stored and disseminated, it was archaic.

In 1982 a concerted effort was made to share professional materials and create an educational resource system which could benefit off-campus students all over the state. Not just CCV, but also off-campus students from Johnson, Castleton, and Vermont Technical College were able to benefit from the preliminary efforts to collect and store information relevant to the classes they were taking in local communities. The system still awaits full development and implementation.

VSC library development plans are important to CCV. In the proposed system, each student will have access to a single, joint on-line catalog in a network which includes the libraries of Castleton State College, Johnson State College, Lyndon State College, and Vermont Technical College as well as the University of Vermont, Middlebury

College and the State Department of Libraries. It also means participation in a joint serials list, increased use of on-line searching, and digital facsimile transceivers in each of three CCV regional offices. At some time in the near future, through automation, each CCV student, instructor and staff member may be able to know what all VSC libraries hold and have on order. Interlibrary loan within the joint system should improve in efficiency and volume. In summary, automation will provide some of the answers to how the college can provide access to information and materials not normally available locally.

CCV's initial attempt to implement the VSC goal of insuring that all graduates will be able to make efficient and effective use of information resources has led to the formation of a Resource Task Force designed to help students, instructors and staff do effective research.

Formed in the summer of 1984, the Task Force will publish a *Resource/Bibliographic Instruction Manual* in March 1985. It will complement the college's degree program manual which sets the following expectation for students' research skills:

1. develop appropriate topics or questions as a basis for the research;
2. locate and use resource materials such as library catalogs, bibliographies, indexes, abstracts, and computer databases; and,
3. set up a research paper in correct form using an outline, footnotes, and a bibliography.

The manual will cover the following topics in order to help students develop these skills:

1. The self-reliant learner: The essential difference between CCV and many other colleges lies in what CCV believes about education and learning, and most particularly, in what it believes about students. Self-reliant learners are people who can assess what they know and what they need to learn; they can use learning skills; and they can plan their studies to meet educational and career goals. In short, they are in charge of their own learning.
    a. What is the importance of research to this goal
    b. What are the expectations for the college-educated person
2. The reasons for seeking information
    a. How does one form a research question

  b. What is the relationship between research questions and the
     individual quest for knowledge
3. What is information
  a. How information is collected and disseminated in our
     society
  b. Common sources of information: libraries, other
     organizations, human resources
4. What are the skills one develops for finding information
  a. Description of research methods and search strategies
  b. The difference between quantitative versus qualitative
     research
5. The appropriate uses and some of the misuses of information
  a. A description of the concepts of copyrights and fair use
  b. A discussion of academic honesty, scholarly apparatus, and
     plagiarism
6. The particular skills needed for library research
  a. The differences between high school and college libraries
  b. How interlibrary loan systems operate
  c. A description of OCLC and other search systems
7. Some of the strategies to use in the library
  a. Familiarity with common reference materials
  b. The use of catalogs and cataloging systems
  c. Ways to use library resources to both formulate and answer
     research questions
8. The relevant aspects of computerization and databases
9. A glossary of terms related to information, research, and
   libraries
10. Sample diagram of a local resource information center
11. Index

The library manual will be approximately fifty pages, and designed to
be used by all CCV degree students as part of a course entitled
"Degree Planning Seminar." This seminar is designed to take students
step-by-step through the process of developing an individualized
degree.   In addition, it will be strongly recommended as a
supplementary resource in selected curriculum offerings. The manual
will further strengthen the institution's philosophy that education is an
on-going process and that a student's studies help with the
development of thinking and learning skills. It is designed to help
students determine how they learn best, and how to locate the
appropriate resources for learning.

Since the VSC system plan is based on the notion of sharing information state-wide, it is important for CCV to find ways of collecting, classifying, and making available for use the educational resources employed by staff, instructors, and students throughout the state. The college has attempted to develop an internal supplementary resource system to include a collection of college-level textbooks, programmed materials, occupational and career journals and newspapers, filmstrips, slides, *ERIC* microfiche, audiovisual equipment, catalogs of books, films located at other institutions, bibliographies and staff development materials. The attempts have failed primarily because once collected and classified, the educational resources rested in their respective locations never to be resurrected. The present Resource Task Force hopes that an automated system using Zenith 100 computers, and an Infostar database will allow the staff to enter and retrieve data efficiently and conveniently, and that the system will be used daily throughout the state.

The college's instructional resource system rests on the assumption that much information related to instructional effectiveness has been collected college-wide, and much more needs to be collected, classified and made available for distribution. A computerized system for accomplishing this task is sorely needed. The content is to be used primarily to improve instructional methods in every CCV class throughout the state, particularly in those rural and economically deprived areas which might otherwise have no access to current educational resources.

The system can be described as:

1. Easy to use, requiring minimal staff training to input and access information
2. Equally available to students, instructors and staff in all site offices
3. Classified by use of Library of Congress subject headings
4. Reviewed, updated and changed easily
5. Designed to encourage search strategies
6. Not coordinator-dependent
7. Having the capacity to transmit a file
8. Interfaced with a broader-based communications system
9. Preserving hierarchical sorts while having clear, simple points of entry
10. Storing course as well as topical information

The general structure of the CCV database system will include CONTENT, FORM, USE, IDENTIFICATION and ANNOTATION. Information will be entered and sorted in a variety of fields and a user manual will be prepared to ensure early success. The process will be structured to encourage an increasing sophistication in search strategies. In the ideal, the system will have tutorial capacity.

Members of the Resources Task Force have developed a format to be used for entering data into the file. There now remains the task of collecting information currently on hand, entering the site office. The staff is hopeful that the system will grow to be a useful and exciting learning tool for the entire college community. It will allow users to share "best teaching practice techniques" in standardized college courses throughout the state. Since the college's collections are particularly rich in books and articles related to current theory on adult learning, this material should be shared throughout the greater VSC system as part of CCV's continuing efforts to contribute as well as use resources in the larger network.

In addition to the publication of a library manual and development of a computerized resource file, the college is planning to build small reference collections in each of its site offices. Plans and funding for this project have been outlined in the VSC Task Force Report. It will be the next task of the Community College Task Force to plan for the selection and purchase of those collections as well as cataloging. Increased reference service is to include two reference librarians for the college.

Inclusion in the Vermont State College system's plans for library development has monumental implications for the Community College of Vermont. Working alone to raise the funds for automation would make it impossible for the college to share in a state library network. Combining its efforts with four other colleges makes possible the impossible dream of securing the educational resources to provide equal opportunity throughout the state to all of the students who wish to take CCV courses. It means that instructors in small communities can do the research necessary to prepare for and teach their courses. It means that staff at a reasonable cost, and with a minimal amount of inconvenience can work toward improving the college curriculum. In summary, it means that the college community can work continually to improve the quality and quantity of its course offerings to those rural, disadvantaged Vermonters for whom the college was founded.

Note

[1] The paper prepared by Mr. Lindberg and Ms. Chalfoun was presented at the second Off-campus Library Services Conference, Knoxville, Tennessee and appeared in the 1986 edition of the conference proceedings. Additional information about this off-campus library services program was provided by these authors in articles prepared for the third and fourth Off-campus Library Services Conferences.

Chalfoun, E. (1987). Off-campus Library Services of the Community College of Vermont. In B.M. Lessin (Ed.), *The Off-campus Library Services Conference Proceedings* (pp.75-81).   Mount Pleasant, MI: Central Michigan University Press.

Lindberg, D.L. (1987).   Why Automation: Getting Information Technology Off-campus.   In B.M. Lessin (Ed.), *The Off-campus Library Services Conference Proceedings* (pp.194-199).   Mount Pleasant, MI: Central Michigan University Press.

Chalfoun, E. (1989).   After Automation -- What Next? In B.M. Lessin (Ed.), *The Off-campus Library Services Conference Proceedings* (pp.71-77).   Mount Pleasant, MI: Central Michigan University.

Library Support for Off-campus Graduate Professional Programs at Domestic and International Sites[1]

H. Maynard Lowry

Introduction

This paper discusses the challenges of meeting the library resource needs of students working toward graduate professional degrees through study at off-campus sites. The instructional environment for the respective programs offered by Loma Linda University's schools of Education and Public Health are distinctly different. The School of Education program, while off-campus, more nearly approximates traditional on-campus instruction. The program offered by the School of Public Health is more consistent with non-traditional off-campus programs. Each school offers its programs at domestic and international sites. The programs of the two schools are compared and contrasted and the problems and solutions developed for providing library resources to the enrolled students are discussed.

Off-Campus Programs and University Mission

The off-campus programs offered by Loma Linda University have typically attracted working professionals who wish to upgrade their professional skills and credentials. The off-campus programs of the two schools have been centered at nearly a dozen domestic sites. For nearly a decade both the schools of Education and Public Health, have offered extended campus programs at several international sites. These programs developed largely out of an institutional mission to support the educational and professional education needs of personnel working in a world-wide system of educational and health care facilities operated by the Seventh-day Adventist denomination. Loma Linda University is the largest and most educationally diverse institution operated by this denomination and it has a long history of direct international service and indirect service through its graduates.

The University's most visible programs are in the health sciences. Of its ten schools, five have a health science focus--medicine, dentistry, allied health, nursing and public health. The University also offers an undergraduate liberal arts program in addition to graduate programs in business and education. Instruction in the latter area extends through the doctoral level.

The University is accredited by some twenty professional accrediting bodies in addition to the regional, Western Association of Schools and Colleges. The School of Public Health is accredited by the American Public Health Association. The School of Education has chosen to seek no professional accreditation beyond that granted by the regional association and the certification of programs approved by the State of California, Commission on Teacher Credentialing.

Course Format and Delivery

The delivery format for courses offered by the two schools differ. The School of Education uses a traditional delivery format with on-site instruction by university faculty at host sites. These host instructional sites are located at three accredited, North American, postsecondary educational institutions. Each has an adequate library collection to support its institutional mission and each holds materials in education and the related social sciences areas to support its own undergraduate teacher education programs. The two international sites where the School of Education has established off-campus programs are also located at postsecondary institutions and have established library resources.

The delivery of course instruction for the programs of the School of Education resembles an on-campus summer program. Depending upon the course, instruction generally extends over a two to five week period with credit being granted proportional to the number of contact hours during the period of instruction. Loma Linda University faculty and qualified local adjunct faculty present traditional classroom instruction and make educational assignments which are similar to those completed in any on-campus program. The off-campus educational program focuses on preparation in elementary education and administration. The program's requirements include completion of forty-five quarter hours of prescribed and elective academic work and successful completion of a comprehensive examination. Students enrolled in the program are generally employed elementary school teachers who hold the baccalaureate degree, but who wish advanced academic preparation.

The School of Public Health uses a non-traditional instructional format which incorporates independent study as well as concentrated classroom instruction. Most courses extend over a ten-week period. Each course begins with a period of four-to-five weeks of independent study centered readings and exercises outlined in a class syllabus. With the completion of preliminary course readings the students are prepared to discuss these during the intensive classroom experience which occurs at the midpoint in the course. Students assemble at a central location for an intensive three-to-four day instructional session with School of Public Health faculty. With few exceptions, the instructor responsible for presenting the course on-campus also presents the instruction to off-campus students. Students have the same number of face-to-face instructional hours with the faculty member as do on-campus students. In this way a level of consistency and continuity is maintained between on-campus and off-campus courses.

Following the lecture and discussion meetings with the professor and during the remaining period of the course students complete other course requirements. These generally include written research papers. Generally student progress is also evaluated with end of course proctored examinations, similar to those given to on-campus students. The program focuses on two areas of public health--health promotion and health administration.

All enrolled students are adults and most are health professionals (mainly nursing, nutrition and other allied health professions). Each must complete forty-eight credits of course work for completion of the degree. Others without a background in one of the health professions may enroll in a sixty-credit program.

International Instructional Sites

The development of programs at international sites is a relatively recent development. The School of Education recently introduced new off-campus programs in Australia and Costa Rica. A Canadian site has been in existence since 1981. The School of Public Health has offered programs in Canada, Singapore, Haiti, Columbia, Jamaica, and Mexico. At the present time the Haiti site is the only one in operation.

With the increasing interest of developing countries in technical and health education, other inquires and requests to establish additional off-campus sites have come to the University from several national governments. The primary interest has been to upgrade the education of health professionals in areas of health administration and health education.

While the instructional delivery format for the two schools mentioned above remains relatively consistent between the domestic and foreign sites, there are significant and contrasting problems. At the international sites these generally involve language and access to instructional materials. Access to appropriate library resources is a particular problem in the non-English speaking countries. Classroom translators are often necessary. While instruction is given in English in Columbia, a majority of the students use Spanish as their working language. A similar problem exists in Haiti where the working language of the students is French.

Some factors that are acknowledged as strengths in the off-campus program in North America are considered assets in the international program as well. These factors include: [a] a student group comprised of mature working professionals committed to the need for the program and motivated to complete a program of independent and directed study; and [b] grouping of students who progress through the program together. The intensive instructional sessions provide a shared experience and point of focus for students. They have a place to exchange views and experiences and a forum to discuss and analyze applied problems. Finally [c] the course format, including the intensive instruction and independent student work, meets the requirements of working professionals who have limited access to similar educational opportunities in their own countries.

In contrast to the strengths and benefits of the program, there are recognized weaknesses as well. These weaknesses include: [a] the lack of ready access to instructors from the beginning of the students' learning experience and throughout the instructional experience; and [b] a feeling among some students that they face personal/academic risk at not being able to size up the instructor outside the brief mid-course encounter. Finally [c] there is a relatively limited access to library materials for the completion of assignments and outside research.

From an academic perspective evaluation of program results have been limited; however, a formal comparison of students performance in the public health statistics course shows no significant difference in the performance of on-campus students and off-campus students at domestic sites. No similar evaluation has yet been conducted at the international sites.

Library Role and Support

Similar to the experience of others, the programs described here were initiated by the respective schools without much prior consideration of the library resource needs of students. But, several factors have worked together to incorporate a larger role for the University Libraries in this program. The concern of the schools for library resources has become a more salient issue for at least three reasons. First, the instructional intent of the program is to produce student learning and mastery of content that is similar to what is achieved in the on-campus format. Therefore, access to library resources has become an indispensable part of the program. Students have expressed this need for access to library materials and have welcomed the efforts of the University Libraries to meet these needs.

Second, the entry of state licensing commissions into the educational review and evaluation process in the respective jurisdictions where the programs operate has increased institutional awareness of the need for readily available library resources to support off-campus instruction.

The broad development of off-campus educations programs is a relatively recent development in many institutions. The expressed regional and professional accrediting agencies' concern for the academic quality and educational services available to these students in these programs is a relatively recent development. The rapid growth of such programs has caused accrediting groups to express their expectations in more concrete terms through formal guidelines and standards.

The accrediting and licensing agency mandates, as well as a growing faculty awareness, have created an opportunity for the libraries to take an active role in the off-campus programs. The dialogue about library services has included both the faculty and the librarians at the host site libraries. In addition to this dialogue, the shared experiences of librarians in other institutions supporting off-campus programs have been invaluable in developing library service strategies and procedures.

Discussions with faculty and program coordinators have focused on several needs. Among these are the local availability of library resources specific to the courses being taught. To adequately meet this need it has been recognized that advance planning is necessary. Course bibliographies obtained from the faculty responsible for the courses have been the starting point. Existing course bibliographies have been collected. Entries have been searched on OCLC and downloaded to disk. Using the Personal Bibliographic Systems (PBS), Bibliolink software, the raw data have been transformed into a data format usable by PBS' ProCite. ProCite is a "bibliographic information management system...designed specifically for organizing bibliographic references." With this tool it has been possible to prepare master author and subject bibliographies of all materials contained in the course bibliographies. It was found that in some cases, course bibliographies had not been updated to reflect recent relevant publications. This library review of course bibliographies thus became the basis for assisting faculty in updating their course bibliographies.

One stipulation of the instructional contracts with the host institutions that cooperate with the School of Education, has been that a fixed per cent of the contract payment will be specifically assigned to purchase local library materials. The course bibliographies have been used at the host sites as the basis for making these collection development decisions. In addition, the University Library has been given the responsibility for monitoring the expenditure of these funds at the host institutions. The librarians at the host sites have been requested to file a bibliography of newly acquired books related to education with the Loma Linda University Library at the end of each fiscal year.

A student handbook prepared for students in the School of Education and School of Public Health off-campus programs has been a valuable tool to create an awareness of library services. The handbook contains a three-page section describing the resources of the Loma Linda University Libraries and the procedures for requesting materials and information. Access throughout North America is by a toll-free number.

Students are also encouraged to determine the extent of local library resources which may be useful in their studies. With the cooperation of the Office of Extended Programs in the School of Public Health, the University Libraries recently began to take a more proactive role in assisting students with the identification of local library resources.

Each student is expected to take the initiative in determining the availability and adequacy of local library resources to meet his/her needs. Each student, upon initial enrollment in the extended campus program, is required to complete a "library use plan." The plan requires that the student investigate and list those libraries with appropriate collections that are located within convenient distance from the student's home. The student is also required to indicate whether a user fee is required of non-affiliated users. Up to half the cost (to a maximum of $25 per course) of library service fees are reimbursed to the student. When completed, the plan also provides data for the University Library to contact the respective libraries to introduce the student and make whatever arrangements may be necessary to assure that the student has library access.

The National Library of Medicine coordinates a nationwide biomedical communication network of academic health science libraries organized into seven regions. In addition to a regional library in each of the seven areas, secondary level "resource libraries" exists within each region. Many of these are connected directly with medical schools or large medical centers. These libraries in turn support a tertiary level network of hospital libraries as well as independent health professionals who have no direct access to adequate library facilities.

The "resource libraries" take an active role in promoting biomedical information access. Among the services provided are reference, interlibrary loan, and on-line searching. Regional bibliographic tools and union lists of serials have been developed in most regions to facilitate resource sharing. Of particular value to students who may inquire about possible local resources is a listing of the information services available from each of the "resource libraries." These libraries provide a full range of information services to non-affiliated health professionals on request.

Library Support for International Programs

Assuring that students have access to adequate library resources at international instructional sites has been the largest challenge of the off-campus educational program. The adequacy of access to library resources is often dependent upon the country in which students live and work. In general, Canadian students have reported few problems in securing adequate library resources.

One instructional goal is to make the course of study relevant to particular national or regional context of the students. To promote this goal faculty have encouraged students to avoid American perspectives on particular problems and to seek out relevant information from the respective national or regional perspective. The library research problems that have been encountered have usually been related to the completing papers which deal with these local health and environmental problems. Often scientific literature has not been well developed on unique national and regional health and environmental problems.

While the library resources are available in the larger urban centers and especially in the national capitals, these resources may not be available to students who come from locations at some distance from these centers.The variety of student experience in obtaining access to adequate library materials is pointed up in the comments of one student who lived and worked in both Hong Kong and Singapore during the period of his study. He expressed satisfaction with the adequacy of library resources available to him, but said that students working in and traveling to the Singapore site from more remote locations had considerable difficulty in locating some materials. In some cases, materials brought by the respective teachers to the lecture site were of assistance to these students.

With the School of Education program and the assistance provided by the libraries at the host sites, the Libraries have concentrated on enhancing resources and otherwise supporting the libraries at these sites. But the School of Public Health program does not rely on the libraries of host institutions as the School of Education program does. Few of the Public Health students studying at international sites are actually close enough to adequately stocked libraries. As previously noted, faculty have attempted to transport copies of articles and books to the international sites to compensate for the access problem. However, this solution is fraught with some ethical and legal problems involving copyright. In some cases language is also a problem.

Delivery systems that have been considered include international mail and other similar means. However, cost and reliability of mail delivery presents considerable obstacles. Except to Canada, the cost of airmail is forty-five cents per half ounce. Surface mail is slow and can seldom be expected to meet the time frame and requirements of the enrolled students. The delays and the cost of mail service have been considered disabling objections to this mode of delivery. The declining cost of telefacsimile transmission has helped to improve access. While still expensive, telefacsimile transmission provides both prompt and more reliable access than can be provided by mail.

At international sites the additional problem of language exists. Teaching and interacting with student through interpreters is a less than preferred condition for instructors in the off-campus program. But in addition, faculty face the challenge of obtaining appropriate textbooks and readings in the students preferred languages of French and Spanish. With a collection development policy which prefers English language materials, the needed materials in Spanish and French are seldom available from the University Libraries. In many cases translations or equivalent materials do not exist.

The Libraries have recently attempted to enlarge their assistance and support at the international instruction sites. This has been considerably easier where a host institution and fixed library site exists. The first step taken by the Libraries was to send a member of the professional staff to the international off-campus sites to access the availability of resources. This had given the Libraries a more accurate picture of host site resources as well as the resources of other areas libraries. These visits have provided the librarians with an opportunity to share professional perspectives on needs of the off-campus and to work together to solve some of the information delivery problems. The international site visits have also provided the librarians with a more accurate picture of the extent and possibility of local cooperative arrangements with area libraries. Interlibrary cooperation and expectations of open access that prevail in the United States can not necessarily be assumed to apply elsewhere.

The library staff have begun to gather information on sources of foreign language materials. Large bibliographic utilities like OCLC have been particularly useful in this task. Using the CD ROM subset of the OCLC database for Educational Materials in Libraries, it has been possible to isolate more than 16,000 cataloged titles in Spanish on topics related to education. The newly implemented EPIC service from OCLC provides an even more up-to-date source of information. Using course bibliographies and LC subheadings assigned to materials for individual classes items it has been possible to prepare lists of Spanish materials that may have value in the program in Costa Rica. Selected materials can then be recommended for library purchase at that site.

Meeting the needs of students for current journals at international sites has been a lingering problem. In some cases, translations of English language materials have been arranged. However, this does little to assist students who require access to materials for independently researched papers.

Closing Thoughts

Providing adequate library service to support graduate and professional students in an international context is a challenging undertaking. It involves issues of both international education and international librarianship. Developing library services which will meet the needs of international students in particular is likely to be more a product of trial and error and evolution rather than planning and design at this stage. Little guidance is available from the library literature or from the experience of others at this point.

Providing library services for students at domestic sites is less problematic because of the experience, reports and solutions developed and offered by a growing number of institutions involved in such programs. Practice is often enhanced by feedback from licensing agencies and by the peer evaluation process of accreditation.

Significant problems continue to elude solution for the present. These problems include providing access to materials in the language of instruction and timely delivery of current library materials to individuals working on research projects at international sites. However, the educational mission of the University and the related obligation to support international development and education are sufficient reasons for persistence and for continuing efforts to seek solutions to these information access problems. New technologies have made some contribution to solving these problems. But, the problems should not be considered daunting as the goal of supporting international educational development is pursued.

Note

[1] Mr. Lowry's paper was presented at the fourth Off-campus Library Services Conference, Charleston, South Carolina, and appeared in the 1989 edition of the conference proceedings.

Academic Librarians in the Field:
Library Service to Off-campus Students[1]

Stephanie Rogers Bangert

St. Mary's College of California is a Catholic liberal arts college founded in San Francisco in 1863. The college moved to its current 420 acre site in Moraga, a suburban community in Contra Costa County about thirty minutes' drive from San Francisco, in 1928. The college is owned and operated by the Institute of the Brothers of the Christian Schools. A Christian Brother and lay staff comprise the current campus faculty of 163, and the additional 197 faculty who support graduate and off-campus programs. Twenty-five baccalaureate programs and five graduate programs are offered to campus students. The School of Extended Education offers two baccalaureate programs and two graduate programs to off-campus adult learners.

St. Mary's College has a total enrollment of 3,171 students: 2446 undergraduates and 725 graduates (Fall 1985). Of these, 609 are off-campus Extended Education students. (The student population of the college has experienced a dramatic increase: since 1970 the enrollment has more than tripled.) Approximately 900 of the college's undergraduates now reside on campus.

The population of Contra Costa County by the year 2000 is expected to be 845,000, up twenty percent from the current figure. While faculty and administration are discussing the issue of future institutional size, it is clear that local demographics may influence St. Mary's overall character and, quite possibly, impact the college's educational goals.

The Library

St. Albert Hall Library, constructed in 1968, houses a collection of 154,500 volumes. The library has a professional staff of 7.75 FTE (full time equivalent) librarians: the Library Director, Assistant Director for Information Services, Assistant Director for Collection Development, Technical Services and Cataloging Librarian, .5 FTE Special Collections Librarian, and 3.25 FTE Information Services Librarians. With increasing demand for more sophisticated library services, e.g. computerized reference, library instruction to undergraduate and graduate classrooms, and research support for off-campus students, the number of the library's professional staff has grown accordingly. The number of support staff positions is 4.75 FTE; approximately 2.0 FTE students are employed annually.

The role of the library at St. Mary's College has evolved from book repository to functional study hall to interactive information center. Over time, it has been the patterns of library use which have contributed to and precipitate change in the library's role. St. Mary's College once focused on providing a liberal arts education to young men residing on campus. The college library supported a curriculum heavily oriented toward primary resource material, i.e., the Great Books tradition, and was a repository for multiple copies of textbooks. Today, the college is providing a diversity of degree programs to both men and women. It also provides education for the generalist or specialist, the recent high school graduate, or re-entry adult learner. The library now attempts to support a complex curriculum requiring both theoretical and practical resource material.

The library has an active user education program where reference librarians provide classroom instruction (on and off-campus) in research strategy. Computerized literature searching via the DIALOG and BRS information retrieval systems as required by many graduate and Extended Education programs, is performed by the professional staff. Document delivery and expedited interlibrary borrowing services are now available to access materials not owned by St. Mary's College. Information referral and exchange with a variety of local, special, public, and academic libraries is performed on a regular basis.

Information services are no longer limited to undergraduate students who reside on campus. Our graduate and Extended Education programs attract adult professionals, many of whom are local business executives. These students make use of the library on nights and weekends. (Approximately six percent of the off-campus Extended Education students use the campus library.) Because St. Mary's is the only four year college in Central Contra Costa County, it is viewed by many local residents as the largest information resource east of Berkeley. Students from other institutions of higher education make use of our library regularly, and new businesses in Contra Costa County have also emerged as part of our changing and growing clientele.

School of Extended Education

Academic programs in St. Mary's College's Division of Extended Education began in 1975. The dean of this new division was appointed in 1978 and in 1984 the division was officially reorganized as the School of Extended Education. Since 1975, over three thousand students have earned their baccalaureate or master's degrees, and over six hundred have completed other professional studies. Extended Education offers four degree programs: (a) Master of Science in Health Services Administration; (b) Master of Procurement and Contract Management; (c) Bachelor of Arts in Health Services Administration; and (d) Bachelor of Arts in Management. A certificate program in Paralegal Studies is also offered. Over six hundred off-campus students are enrolled in these programs each year. All classes are held in the evening. The average program length is fourteen months. Students (ages 25-60) are recruited within a hundred mile radius of San Francisco. Most classes are organized in San Francisco, Oakland, San Jose, Stockton, and Sacramento. Many classes now, however, are being organized in suburban communities such as Walnut Creek, San Rafael, Napa, and Salinas.

In 1980, the Western Association of Schools and Colleges (WASC) conducted an extensive review of the college. In the WASC final report to the College, the following specific recommendation was made to the administration regarding library service to its non-traditional programs: "...the Team recommends that the college make library and other learning resources available to all off-campus students at appropriate locations."

This recommendation set into motion the development and subsequent implementation of a unique library program which now fulfills the research, access, and bibliographic instruction needs of St. Mary's College off-campus students.

Library Service to the School of Extended Education

Staffing

Two years following the 1980 WASC report a full-time professional librarian position, the benefits of which were to be shared equally by the college library and the School of Extended Education, received administration approval. In April 1983, the Special Services Librarian was hired to design, implement, and manage library services to off-campus students. Since that time, the School of Extended Education has subsidized an increase in librarian staff from .5 FTE to 1.25 FTE. The Special Services Librarian was promoted to Assistant Director for Information Services in 1985 and currently maintains administrative responsibility over the extended Education library program. The Assistant Director manages and supervises reference, automation, access (circulation and interlibrary loan), and extended service activities within the college library. Two reference librarians, who report to the Assistant Director, provide the "field" library service to Extended Education programs. One librarian is an on-campus .5 FTE librarian, the other is based off-campus and is at .25 FTE. The campus librarian holds a full-time joint position between the library and the School of Extended Education as does the Assistant Director. The off-campus librarian is contracted on an hourly basis. Field librarians provide the majority of class site visits, in-person reference interviews, and the execution of computer searches. The Assistant Director, who once performed field librarian responsibilities, now supervises professional staff, evaluates service quality, and communicates with the Dean of the School and division directors on budget and planning issues. As the campus librarian continues to increase her involvement in curricular support and collection development for the Extended Education programs, it is likely that an additional .25 FTE will be required to assist in local class visits, computer searching, and individualized reference assistance.

In the past, the library has contributed a modest number of student employee hours to handle clerical responsibilities. However, with the dramatic increase in interlibrary loan business, it is anticipated that the School will fund a student position (ten to fifteen hours/week) in the next fiscal year.

Success of the library service program and its ability to meet information needs of Extended Education is primarily attributed to the field librarian concept. The blend of a permanent staff position with a contracted field position has given the Extended Education librarian team the flexibility to accommodate teaching responsibilities for forty-five evening classes per year in geographical areas ranging 5-100 miles from the Moraga campus. The campus librarian can also assume more administrative responsibilities, e.g., establish a consistent rapport with Extended education staff and faculty. The contracted field librarian, on the other hand, can take on special projects requiring flexibility, such as providing extra tours of Bay Area libraries, selecting and installing microcomputer equipment in both library and field office locations, attending professional development workshops, and then repackaging the information for college librarian staff. Contracting an off-campus librarian also allows for change should Extended Education re-evaluate their library service needs in the future.

Description of Service

The scope of service to all degree programs includes on-site class visits to both campus and off-campus students. Visits are provided to all geographical locations where classes are organized. Service to programs also includes personalized reference assistance both in-person and over the telephone, tours of local library facilities, expedited interlibrary borrowing and document delivery, and related information referral. Service to the paralegal program has included infrequent computer searching as well as occasional class visits to demonstrate the DIALOG Information Retrieval System. Support to the marketing division of Extended Education has involved several field librarian visits to student orientation meetings. Service to Extended Education faculty and staff entails computer searching, research assistance, citation verification, and interlibrary borrowing.

Table 1

Librarian Time by Type of Service to School of Extended Education

Academic Year 1985/1986

	On-campus Extension Ed. Librarian	Off-campus Extension Ed. Librarian
Reference Assistance	35%	15%
Class Visits	30%	20%
Curricular support & Materials Preparation	20%	30%
Collection Development	10%	5%
Meetings and Professional Dev.	5%	30%

Users

Users for the off-campus library services program are derived from one of the following divisions in the School of Extended Education: Extended Education Degree Programs (EEDP), Procurement and Contract Management, or Paralegal. The primary focus of library service the first year (1983) was to the Extended Education Degree Programs. At that time, EEDP offered two baccalaureate degree programs: Health Service Administration, and Management. A master's degree in Health Services Administration was offered beginning 1984. Off-campus library service was provided to the Procurement program in 1984 and to the Paralegal program in 1985. Some promotional support is currently given to the Extended Education Marketing division. Although the majority of service is provided to the students of these programs, their faculty and staff are eligible for service as well.

Table 2

School of Extended Education Use of Library Service by Type of User, Program, and Year

Category and Number of Users	1983/84	1984/85	1985/86
Health Services (Bachelor's Program)	65	54	55
Management (Bachelor's Program)	56	99	106
Procurement & Contract Mgmt. (Master's Program)	11	7	18
Health Services (Master's Program)			31
Paralegal (Professional Studies)		3	
Faculty - all programs	3	10	5
Staff - all programs	1	21	13

Total users seen: 1983/84, 136; 1984/85, 194; 1985/86, 228.

Class Visits

Faculty and student feedback suggests that on-site class visits by library staff provide the single most significant link between Extended Education students and the learning resources of St. Mary's College. Information referral and resource networking with other San Francisco Bay Area libraries provides a further link between students and library centers in geographical proximity to home or classroom.

Table 3

Librarian Class Visits to School of Extended Education by Year

Category & Number of Classes	1983/84	1984/85	1985/86
Health Services (Bachelor's)	9	11	12
Management (Bachelor's)	17	19	26
Health Services (Master's)		1	3
Procurement & Contract Mgmt. (Master's Program)		2	1
Paralegal (Professional Studies)	3	2	3

Total number of classes provided: 1983/84, 29; 1984/85, 35; 1985/86, 45.

In the classroom, the 1½-2 hour librarian presentation describes a step-by-step methodology for the research process. A summary of the major reference sources in a given field is covered. Computerized literature searching is discussed, followed by policy, procedure, and organizational issues of local academic, public, and special libraries. Working with EEDP program directors, the campus librarians determined that the thirteenth week of the bachelor programs was the appropriate time for the site visit in the curriculum.

The master's programs have placed the class visit somewhat earlier in the curriculum. A subject-oriented pathfinder and bibliography was prepared for the Health Services Administration, Management, and Procurement programs. It was distributed to students via the course syllabus. All handouts follow a recommended five-step strategy to simplify the research process:

Step 1. Define your topic
Step 2. Gain a general overview
Step 3. Locate references to documents
Step 4. Locate the documents
Step 5. Read and take notes

(This outline for the research process has now been integrated into all college library bibliographic publications.)

Research and Reference Assistance

In the Management and Health Services Administration programs students are required to complete a course entitled "The Project." Students are asked to design and implement a work-related project based upon an analytical model of goal setting, problem identification, data collection and evaluation. As part of the intensive two hundred hour project design phase, students are required to conduct a comprehensive review of the literature. At least fifteen sources are to be located, reviewed, and synthesized. References can be derived from journals, books, government documents, newspapers, statistical and other factual data. Use of computer-stored and other non-print resources is encouraged.

The purpose of the librarian class visit is to introduce students to the research and process and to orient students to appropriate libraries in their geographical location. Individual reference assistance is the next step for students requiring additional help in research topic definition, the identification of relevant information sources, preparation for computerized literature search, and referral to other library collections. Those students requesting individual reference assistance usually do so three-to-five weeks following the librarian visit. Reference assistance is available by appointment for in-person interviews, telephone, and electronic mail.

Fifty-one percent of all Extended Education students attend classes in Contra Costa County and the Greater East Bay--a 15-20 mile radius of the St. Mary's College campus. Many of these students elect later to meet with the Extended Education librarian who works in the college library. Even with this proximity to the campus, some students prefer a telephone reference interview and follow-up call. Thirty-three percent of Extended Education students attend classes organized 40-60 miles away from the college's Moraga campus. Most of these classes are located in the South Bay. One off-campus librarian maintains her office in the San Jose area in conjunction with the Extended Education Marketing division. Most South Bay students requiring individual reference assistance will choose to meet with the field librarian in-person. The remaining sixteen percent of Extended Education students attend classes in San Francisco and the North Bay--a 20-60 mile radius from the St. Mary's campus. Very few classes are held outside a sixty mile radius. In all cases, most students elect to contact Extended Education librarians by telephone.

During the first year of service students primarily contacted librarians for computer searches. Students now are more likely to request both personalized reference assistance as well as computer searches. Two factors have contributed to the change in type of reference assistance requested:

1. faculty and librarians encourage students to gain a general overview of the literature before requesting a computer search; and
2. students increasingly use reference materials recommended in the class visit which often decreases or eliminates the need for a computer search altogether.

Table 4

Type of Reference Assistance Provided by Librarian to School of Extended Education

	1983/84	1984/85	1985/86
Computer Search Only	56%	30%	37%
Reference Plus Computer Search	29%	35%	48%
Reference Assistance Only	15%	35%	10%
Computer Search Plus ILL			5%

Individual research and reference assistance to Extended Education students, faculty, and staff consumes considerable librarian time. To satisfy the majority of reference-plus-computer search requests, a one hour appointment is usually necessary. That amount of time has proved adequate to conduct an extensive reference interview, perform a computer search, discuss methods of locating references, and provide pertinent information regarding the use of local libraries. Extended Education librarians are spending twice the previous amount of time providing reference assistance to faculty. The average appointment is fifty minutes. Extended Education staff continue to receive an average forty-five minutes of individualized reference assistance per appointment.

Computer Searching and Interlibrary Borrowing (ILL)

Computer searching provided to the School of Extended Education is a vital component in the library services program. (see Table 1.) From the program's conception in 1983, the Dean of the School expressed his support for the provision of on-line information services to students by stating that each student is entitled to receive one free computer search during the course of the entire program. Dollar maximums were established for each program to aid in the budgeting process. A computer search costing no greater than fifteen dollars is offered to students in the health program; a computer search costing no greater than twenty-five dollars is offered to students in the management, procurement, and paralegal programs. These amounts take into consideration the dollar per minute cost charged by individual database vendors.

Table 5

Number of Computer Searches Performed for School of Extended Education, 1986

	Students	Faculty	Staff
Health Services Management (BA)	54	2	2
Health Services Management (MA)	103	4	2

	Students	Faculty	Staff
Heath Services Procurement (BA)	19	0	0
Health Services Procurement (MA)	21	2	1
Paralegal	2	0	2
Division Total	199	8	7
Program Total	214		

BA refers to bachelor's programs; MA refers to master's programs.

Extended Education librarians search on the DIALOG and BRS information retrieval systems. While the campus librarians perform searches on an RLIN RLG40 terminal configured to access commercial database systems, the South Bay librarian uses an IBM PC AT, Hayes SmartModem, and letter quality printer. DIALOG searching accounts for eighty-seven percent of all searches performed while BRS searching accounts for thirteen percent. (RLIN and ONTYME electronic mail are used primarily during the interlibrary borrowing operation.) Primary databases used for all Extended Education programs are ABI/INFORM, Health Planning and Administration, Management Contents, Newspaper Index, Nursing and Allied Health, Harvard Business Review, and ERIC.

During the 1985/86 academic year, ninety-four percent of Extended Education users who requested some type of reference assistance received a DIALOG or BRS computer search. As the number of the located references to documents increased, so did the demands on the interlibrary borrowing service increase. By the fourth quarter in 1985, Extended Education users represented thirty percent of all St. Mary's ILL clientele. By the second quarter of 1986, Extended Education users represented sixty-two percent of ILL requesters. Several factors contributed to this increase. The college library's ILL operation is now managed by the campus Extended Education librarian. Because of her expertise in regional networking with other Bay Area libraries, she has found that most library-to-library charges for ILL service can be avoided by careful selection of lending libraries. Also, for the first time, a student employee was hired to handle interlibrary loan activity exclusively. With a more efficient ILL operation in place, field librarians increased promotion of the ILL service to Extended Education students during class visits as well as during the computer search reference interview. In previous years most Extended Education students retrieved their own documents; the majority of those students now utilize the St. Mary's College library ILL service for document delivery. Material that must be photocopied is mailed to the majority of Extended Education students.

Orientations and Tours

Once a student has been accepted into one of the EEDP programs, the School's marketing division organizes an orientation meeting for each geographical class cluster. (For example, a class which is organized in San Jose remains together as one class throughout the entire fourteen month program.) During the 1985/86 academic year, the South Bay field librarian attended seven orientation meetings (two for the health program, five for the management program). At these meetings, a summary of library services is described and a general review of local libraries is presented. Students are informed as to when they can expect the librarian class visit. It is believed that this initial brief introduction to an Extended Education librarian serves to promote library services as well as reinforce the School's commitment to an academically-supported curriculum.

At the request of course instructors or students, the field librarian also provides tours of major libraries. These tours are often organized during evening hours different from the Scheduled class time. Seven tours were offered in the 1985/86 academic year (two for the health program, four for the management program, and one for the procurement program). Libraries toured were Stanford University, San Jose State University, and the City of Sunnyvale Public Library (Main Branch). Feedback indicates that these tours were extremely useful in assisting students to refamiliarize themselves with the physical layout of the reference rooms, card catalogs, and periodical indexes for each library.

Curricular Support

Integrating Library Service into the Curriculum

When the library program to the School of Extended Education was in the design stage, the Special Services Librarian worked with EEDP program directors to evaluate student research and information needs related to the requirements described by program curricula. Since the "Project" courses for bachelor's degrees in both Management and Health Services Administration already required a fifty-hour literature review, librarian attention was immediately focused in that area. Once the basic library program was in place for these courses, new application were sought for existing support services to assist in the objectives of each program.

In 1985, one of the courses in the management program had a library-related assignment integrated into its syllabus. The assignment, designed by the campus Extended Education librarian in consultation with the management program director, was written to complement the objectives of the Management Profession course and also to provide an easy, hands-on introduction to library use. Students were asked to explore trends in the management profession by locating recent journal articles. Specific periodical index titles and relevant subject headings were provided to help expedite the search process. The goal of the assignment was to encourage early use of the library, more specifically to encourage use of business reference materials. Students evaluated their library experience and this information was then forwarded to the college library. The field librarian who was scheduled to visit that same class in the project course reviewed the evaluation questionnaires to determine the most frequently used libraries in the geographical area where the class was organized. Problems raised as a result of the library-related assignment were then addressed in greater detail in the librarian class presentation. Overall, the assignment was seen as a successful introduction to the library research process. The assignment gave students an opportunity to test their library use skills while, at the same time, the librarian was given an opportunity to evaluate student skill level prior to lecture preparation.

Collection Development

The quality of the St. Mary's College library collection has undergone extensive evaluation during the last two years with the Extended

Education campus librarian dedicating ten percent of her time to collection development activities. The quality of the library's holdingsin health, management, and procurement is largely a result of her collection review, acquisition recommendations, and liaison work with faculty. Annually, the library allocates approximately two thousand dollars for Extended Education materials. Based upon the librarian's acquisition recommendations, the School of Extended Education generously supplemented the library's materials budget for the past two years. In 1985, $6,900 was contributed to the library's materials budget, and in 1986, the figure was $8,600. These funds were then used to expand the library collection to support the two Extended Education master's degree programs and to reinforce the business reference and periodical collection.

During the summer of 1985, the campus librarian worked in conjunction with the health services administration program director to promote more faculty participation in collection development. A brief questionnaire was sent out to all health services faculty requesting three basic items of information: area of expertise, recommendations for book or reference titles, and recommendations for journal titles. Examples of areas of expertise are law and ethics, health care trends, marketing and economics of health care, and human resources. The questionnaire asked faculty to make no more than five title recommendations in each of the two categories. Faculty were provided with a summary of recent acquisitions as well as a list of health care and nursing journals owned by St. Mary's College (selected management journals were also included). Approximately twenty-five percent of the questionnaires were returned. The library purchased all in-print book titles as well as the majority of journal titles recommended. A follow-up letter was returned to each faculty respondent indicating those titles which were already owned by the college library and those titles ordered in response to their input.

Networking with Other Libraries

The library services program to the School of Extended Education has been designed to assist students in the research process. Even with the extensive individualized assistance provided by field librarians, most students consult local libraries to acquire information or materials not readily obtainable through interlibrary loan or document delivery, and although the library's ILL service has been upgraded, students may still prefer to browse journal collections in-person, check out books directly, or verify document locations in union or COM catalogs without the assistance of a reference librarian.

A library resources handbook, entitled *Guide to Bay Area Libraries*, has been developed to orient students in the uses of library and information centers available in their geographical area. Originally developed by an Extended Education staff member before the library services program was implemented in 1983, the *Guide* has received extensive revision by the current campus librarian.

Part one of the handbook provides students with tips on choosing a library, suggestions for organizing the information search, and reviews the recommended five-step research strategy. (This five-step research strategy is the foundation for the librarian class lecture and is reinforced in subject bibliographies and pathfinders.) Part two is a directory to one hundred Bay Area academic, special, and public libraries which are available for Extended Education student use. The directory lists current library hours and telephone numbers, collection strengths, and circulation policies. Each participating library was informed, prior to inclusion in the directory, of the nature of Extended Education student information needs. The *Guide* is distributed to EEDP students during orientation. Faculty are encouraged to refer to the handbook throughout the program.

Operating Cost

For the 1985/86 academic year, the operating cost required to support the Extended Education library services program was $35,800. (see Table 2.) It must be noted, however, of the 609 students enrolled in Extended Education, only 228 students, staff, and faculty made full use of individualized reference assistance, computer searching, and interlibrary borrowing. (All students benefitted from a librarian class visit, bibliographic handouts, and the *Guide to Bay Area Libraries*). Actual per student costs are extremely difficult to project.

Table 6

Operating Costs for Library Services Program to School of Extended Education, 1986

	Extended Education	Library
Librarian salaries	$27,000	0
Travel (Class visits, tours)	2,000	0
Computer searching	5,000	0
Printing/Copying	300	0
Telephone/Postage	100	200
Interlibrary Loan	0	1,200
Subtotals	$34,400	$1,400
Total cost	$35,800	

Summary

Library service to the School of Extended Education both meets the present information needs of its students and attempts to anticipate additional needs relating to changes in program curricula. The library program has been designed to provide a comprehensive and individualized information service package: one-on-one reference assistance (in-person or via telephone), access to commercial database systems, instruction in research methodology, and document delivery. Networking with regional libraries is accomplished through the publication of the *Guide to Bay Area Libraries* as well as information referral between the St. Mary's College Library and local library facilities. Concentrated collection evaluation in the fields of health services administration, management, and procurement has resulted in an improved college library collection. Student evaluation questionnaires indicate an overall "excellent" rating of the library program. Satisfaction with the service is primarily attributed to the customized nature of the program; what little negative feedback has been received addresses the time and money associated with document delivery.

Library service tailored to a non-traditional off-campus program requires its own budget, a highly qualified professional staff, and an administration committed to excellence in progressive information services. The field librarian concept, as described in this paper, is one arrangement which allows for flexibility in meeting off-campus information needs while at the same time provides for new and varied librarian expertise within the college. The overall impact of the Extended Education library program on the information services in the college library has been extremely constructive. The program demonstrates that with careful planning and communication with faculty and academic staff, a librarian team can implement a service which is highly relevant to the educational goals of a curriculum. Results of a successful library program in turn benefit the entire institution.

Addendum

Four years have passed since the writing of "Academic Librarians in the Field"--a paper presented at the 1986 Off-Campus Library Services Conference, Reno, Nevada. The Saint Mary's College Library continues to provide comprehensive and individualized information service to the students of the School of Extended Education; however, some aspects of service delivery have been changed. The primary change has been the shift back to the home campus as the primary library instruction site in place of extensive field librarian participation in the off-campus classroom. The change was precipitated by the librarians responsible for service delivery to these non-traditional students. An extensive evaluation in consultation with the School's dean and program directors, it was determined that a more direct hands-on library instruction experience *in a library*, rather than in a classroom, would result in greater comprehension and retention of research skills than previously measured. Change in the program is seen as an appropriate response to the real information and instructional needs of these students.

How has the Saint Mary's College environment changed since the 1985/86 academic year? What have library services to the School of Extended Education looked like since then? The following review will highlight the population, services, costs, and administrative considerations in regard to this unique library user group.

In 1985, Saint Mary's College had a total enrollment of 3,171 students: 2,446 undergraduates and 725 graduates. In 1990, total enrollment is 3,663 students: 2,875 undergraduates and 788 graduates. This represents a 15% increase in total enrollment. The School of Extended Education enrollment has increased from 609 to 750 over this same time period, or, an increase of 23%.

The Saint Albert Hall Library, in a effort to expand its services to the growing number of students, has increased more in collection size than in staff size. In 1986, the collection was comprised of 154,500 volumes; today the collection size is 161,916 volumes. The number of periodical titles owned has increased from 814 to 1,021. The library's professional staff has increased by .25 F.T.E. to yield eight F.T.E. librarians (including the Director); one F.T.E. support position has been added to the staff. The primary change in organization has been a redistribution of some professional responsibilities. Overall program review and evaluation resides in the position of Information Services department head and the development, delivery, and coordination of direct service to Extended Education students rests with an Information Services librarian dedicated to this function.

The number of classes visited by a librarian remained about the same following the 1986 study: 44 classes were provided instruction in 1987 and 35 classes in 1988. (Fewer classes were organized in 1988, thus the drop in librarian visits.) The shift to on-campus instruction in 1989 results in 30 in-library instructional sessions for the students in 36 classes. (Note that campus sessions are scheduled to coincide with students' research assignments.) Library instruction continues to be targeted during the time in a program's curriculum where a research project is required. No significant changes in the health services, management, or procurement programs have been noted. However, graduate programs changed from a semester to a quarter calendar.

The library program to Extended Education students has included computer searching, interlibrary borrowing services, and individualized reference assistance in addition to instruction. Changes during the last four years can be observed in these areas as well.

Librarian-assisted computer searches for students continue to be provided and subsidized by the School of Extended Education. As reported in 1986, 214 computer searches were performed. The following year, that number nearly doubled: 414 searches were provided. Although librarians and Extended Education program directors were pleased with the extensive provision of computer searching for their students, the costs associated with this service became prohibitive. For example, by 1987, the School of Extended Education reimbursed the library for over $15,000 worth of DIALOG database searches. As reported previously, the majority of these searches were performed for the business management program.

To help reduce program costs and to enable students to search a relevant database directly, the librarians recommended purchase and installation of the ABI/Inform CD ROM system in 1988. The School of Extended Education partially subsidized the purchase, and an immediate savings of over $7,000 that year was realized. Since the all-time record of 414 librarian-assisted computer searches in 1987, there has been a decline in number of librarian-assisted searches, respectively: 237 searches (1988) and 146 searches (1989). Direct, hands-on searching by students appears more effective and satisfactory. Knowledge and use of ABI/Inform and other CD ROM systems is now a very important part of the hands-on library instruction component.

It was during this time of increases in computer searching that a dramatic impact upon interlibrary borrowing services was also experienced. (The last five years have shown a 400% increase in interlibrary borrowing requests, with Extended Education students the primary users.) In 1987, for example, there were 1,662 requests from Extended Education students for interlibrary assistance. They represented 85% of the total requestor population. In 1988, Extended Education interlibrary requests for service dropped to 71% of the total, or 780 requests. This decrease was attributed to two factors: (1) graduate students on the quarter calendar were constrained by tighter time deadlines and (2) a policy to limit the number of interlibrary requests per student was implemented.

Collection development activity to strengthen book and periodical materials in support of Extended Education programs has continued to grow over the past four years; accreditation reports have been a factor in this collection growth. The 1980 Western Association of Schools and Colleges (WASC) review recommended that the College provide "library and other learning resources available to all off-campus students at appropriate locations," and the 1986 WASC interim report recommended that "high priority should be devoted to the development of library collections that are at a scale appropriate to the

College's graduate programs." (Two Extended Education programs are at the graduate level: Health Services Administration, and Procurement and Contract Management.)

In response to the WASC recommendation, the library conducted an extensive analysis of collection strengths and weaknesses in 1989. The results of the analysis confirmed the library's self-assessment, that, "the circulating book collections in support of graduate programs are inadequate in quality, depth, diversity, and currentness." Reference and periodical collection, "... are somewhat adequate in quality and currentness."

The School of Extended Education, in an effort to support the improvement of collections for its programs, has continued to supplement the library's materials budget by up to $15,000 during fiscal years 1987/88, 1988/89, and 1989/90. Contributions to the library by the School of Extended Education have facilitated rapid improvements in the overall quantity and quality of book and periodical collections which in turn result in substantial benefit to the entire institution. The 25% increase in number of periodical titles since 1986 is in large part due to these subsidies. It should also be noted that in a 1989 WASC follow-up review, no recommendations were made regarding library services or collections. This is perhaps an indication that service improvements to both areas have been acknowledged and considered responsive to identified needs.

In summary, library service to the School of Extended Education continues to provide relevant information services tailored to the adult non-traditional student. Student evaluations between 1988-1989 show a high score in librarian-teacher effectiveness, but, more revealing, a low score on the retention of material covered. An increasing number of students reported "being overwhelmed" by the amount of information to be absorbed and learned. The change to a more interactive, hands-on instructional component is the current attempt to make the information presented more accessible and useful to their research project. The last four years have shown, then, an ability to evaluate and revise library service delivery as user/librarian satisfaction levels vary.

Market data derived from the School of Extended Education shows that current student attitudes suggest a desire to be more physically connected with the home campus. Administrative support for the change to a required on-campus library instructional session was based, in part, upon this newly-expressed student attitude. Also noteworthy is the fact that as Extended Education programs become more visible to the traditional college community, increased understanding of their curriculum and educational outcomes can be anticipated. The library program continues to serve as a bridge between the traditional and non-traditional areas of the institution.

What might be anticipated for the next four-to-five years for the library program to the School of Extended Education? With the development of a campus computer network, a library on-line catalog, and the application of interactive video and hypercard, it can be anticipated that library service to this unique student population will be re-evaluated. Library service may return to the off-campus classroom, or to a remote learning laboratory, where access to a selection of CD ROM database systems (on-site or remote) and other electronic information tools would be available for the independent researcher.

Reference

Seekamp, L.W. (1990). *Guide to Bay Area Libraries and Other Information Sources*. [Moraga, CA]: St. Mary's College Library.

Note

[1] The paper prepared by Ms. Bangert was presented at the third Off-campus library Services Conference, Reno, Nevada, and appeared in the 1987 edition of the conference proceedings. The author gratefully acknowledges Linda Seekamp, Sharon Cline, and the St. Mary's College Extended Education field librarians for their assistance in data collection.

Regional Accreditation Standards and Off-Campus Library Service[1]

Antoinette M. Kania

The purpose of this paper will be to describe the status of regional accreditation standards for academic libraries as they relate to off-campus library services. The research on which this paper is based was conducted as part of a dissertation study entitled *The Development of a Model Set of Regional Accreditation Standards for Academic Libraries* (1984). Although the dissertation focused on academic library standards for regional accreditation in general, data was generated from the study that relates specifically to off-campus library services. The situation the data describes is both revealing and disconcerting.

The purpose of the original study was to develop a model set of regional accreditation library standards which would encompass both qualitative performance measures suggested for local use. The goal was to make to standards more "outcomes" or performance oriented and to differentiate between the standards that ought to be mandatory, professionally obligatory, or simply advisable for accreditation through the use of the verbs "must", "should" or "may."

The project was conducted in two parts. First, a content analysis was performed on the existing academic library standards of the seven regional accreditation commissions of higher education in 1982. Second, three survey instruments were developed and used to collect expert opinion from academic librarians, accreditation standards and in linking these standards to appropriate performance measures.

In performing the content analysis, ten major subject areas and fifty-seven subtopics were identified, reviewed and reorganized in order to develop a cohesive draft of forty-five representative standards. The first survey instrument was developed to solicit expert opinion on this newly created composite set of standards. In the instrument the verbal was to indicate what they felt ought to be the appropriate level of adherence to that standard for regional accreditation for their own type of institution. The sample to receive this instrument was a purposefully selected national group of sixty-five academic library directors with evaluation team experience and regional accreditation staff members. An attempt was made to balance the sample by region (Middle States, North Central, Western, etc.) and by sector, two-year college, four-year college, and university.

The respondents' ratings of the forty-five items in the instrument were gathered and the relative frequency with which the respondents felt that one of the verbals, "must", "should", or "may" was appropriate for each potential standard statement was computed. In all instances, the verbal selected most frequently (by 50% or more of the respondents), became the verb for that standard in the second draft. The second survey instrument to seek their consensus on the reformulated standards which now included nine standards using the verbal "must" and twenty-three, now called guidelines, using the verbals "should" and "may."

The third instrument was actually a request for expert advice on the applicability and practicality of selected library performance measures that had been tentatively linked to the newly developed individual standards and guidelines. Some sixty methods of evaluating libraries against the standards had been identified from the literature. Sixteen experts in the field, selected because they had either developed performance measures themselves or had utilized some of the methods in their own libraries and published the results, were asked to comment critically.

Some of the results of the study are interesting to note. The content analysis indicated that the regional accreditation commissions agreed on only half of the major topics mentioned in their standards and less than 50% of the overall fifty-seven subtopics existed in any one commission's standards. Only 10% of the topics and 9% of the subtopics suggested any output orientation according to DuMont's (1980) systems model definitions for inputs, processes, and outputs.

From the data from the first instrument it appeared that separate standards for each of the college sectors was not warranted. There was a very high level of agreement (96%) among the sectors on the verbals where at least three of the four sectors agreed. All sectors designed approximately 63% of the standards as "should", 33% as "must" and 3% as "may" to indicate the level of adherence to be required.

The overall acceptability rating for the reformulated standards in the second instrument was over 90%, so that the second draft of the standards became the model set. As a result of the third instrument, twenty-four performance measures were substantiated by experts as applicable and reasonably practical to replicate in academic library self-study and evaluation.

It appeared, therefore, from this original study, that academic libraries are being examined through a wide variety of requirements for regional accreditation. The standards against which they are evaluated were found to differ across the region not only in length and style, but also in content by as much as 50%. This turns out to also be true for off-campus library service specifically as we shall see a little later. The standards were also found to be primarily input- and process-oriented with little emphasis given to the outcomes' dimension.

Through this project, it was possible to develop one set of academic library standards that could accommodate the three major library sectors with increased overall content coverage more representative of concerns of practitioners and with greatly increased outcomes' orientation. Library performance measures were identified and verified as applicable to the new standards as well as practical to use in a real library setting.

Although this study dealt with all aspects of regional accreditation library standards, the data that was generated on the individual elements of those standards made for interesting study for our purposes here today particularly in the area of accreditation standards for off-campus library services.

The content analysis of the standards of the seven regional accreditation commissions (there is one commission for each of the six regions with the exception of two in the Western Association of Schools and Colleges) revealed the degree to which off-campus library services were and were not specifically addressed in 1982 when the original study was conducted. Only three of seven commissions, representing only two of six agencies, specifically referred to the need to provide off-campus library services. Two of the commissions who specifically referred to off-campus library services are the Accrediting Commission for Community and Junior Colleges (1989) and the Accrediting Commission for Senior Colleges and Universities (1979) both of the Western Association and both, in fact, utilizing very similar language. Standard 6C of the Commission for Community and Junior

Colleges says that "Learning Resources are readily available and used by staff and students both on and off-campus," (p. 27) and in addition to that, a sub-statement, Standard 6C.3 says that "If off-campus programs exist, provision [is made] for students to have ready access to resource collections or their equivalents as well as the equipment for using these materials."

Standard 5C and 5C.3 of the Commission for Senior Colleges and Universities essentially say the same thing. Both Commissions are, of course, part of the same regional accreditation association.

Standard IV of the Northwest Association of Schools and Colleges, Commission on Colleges (1982), says under Library and Learning Resources that "wherever an institution provides programs, it must demonstrate that library and learning resources, fully adequate to the programs, are conveniently available and used by students and faculty" (p.6).

Since 1982, the Commission on Colleges of the Southern Association of Colleges and Schools, has proposed a major revision of its *Criteria for Accreditation* (Holley, 1983), adding what amounts to as the most comprehensive accreditation standard on off-campus library services to date. Under Section 5, Library, Part 5.2.1, Services, it says that "An institution must provide appropriate library Services at off-campus locations where credit courses are offered to insure that these courses received the same level of library support as that given to equivalent on-campus courses" (p. 73).

The standard does on to suggest the type and quality of library service that may be developed such as a branch library or a contractual arrangement with another library as well as the need for qualified personnel. With the Southern Association's addition of a standard on off-campus services, the number of accreditation commissions to do so will have been increased to just over half.

The academic library standards of the higher education commissions of the three other regions, the Middle States, North Central and New England Associations (1982, 1982, 1980), while making no specific reference to off-campus library services, at least refer in passing to the need for relationships with other libraries for collection enhancement and exchange of learning resources. In these contexts reference to off-campus library services may be implied.

With the relatively minimal requirements in existing regional accreditation standards for the provision of library materials and services for students and faculty at off-campus sites, it is somewhat surprising to note the level of importance placed on that particular standard by not only the practitioners in the field, but also the regional accreditation staff members in their responses to the composite set of standards developed by this author in the original study described earlier. In that study each respondent was asked to provide the verbal "must", "should" or "may" for each standard statement to indicate its degree of importance for institutional accreditation purposes for his own type of institution. Fifty-three percent (53%), or just over half of the respondents, including all sectors (two-year and four-year college, and university library directors and accreditation agency staff), designated the verbal "must" for the standard.

Provision *must* be made for library users in off-campus locations to have adequate access to library resources and equipment.

Thirty-eight percent (38%) of all respondents selected "should" as the appropriate verbal for a grand total of 91% who felt what such services, where indicated, must be required or, at least, considered as professionally obligatory for regional accreditation purposes. Yet today, three out of seven sets of higher education commissions' standards do not even mention that a college or university should provide or consider providing library services for its students enrolled in its off-campus programs.

In fact, of all the sectors, it was the accreditation officials for whom the greatest majority of respondents (80%) selected the verbal "must." That is somewhat incongruous given the facts. Two of the commissions having no library standards for off-campus services indicated that they felt that those services "must" be provided for accreditation purposes. Yet their own agencies don't require them.

In the second instrument, designed to gather opinion on the general acceptability of the reformulated standards based on the responses to the first instrument, only five, or 10%, or the respondents indicated that the standards on off-campus services were "generally unacceptable." Their reasons for feeling that way were included in remarks which spoke to the need for more clarity in wording, the fact that the statement was too strong and the fact that the statement made requirements that were too difficult to attain.

What we find with the regional accreditation standards for academic libraries nationally is an inconsistency regarding required and recommended criteria for accreditation. Commissions of higher education do not seem to agree on what constitutes the major areas to be evaluated so that the libraries in colleges and universities across the country are evaluating themselves and being examined by outsiders against a variety of requirements for accreditation. This became evident through the initial research on this project and was further substantiated when looked at from the specific point of view of our concerns here today, off-campus library services.

Colleges and universities have continued to develop and increase their program offerings at off-campus sites, and academic libraries have been attempting to address their users' needs at those locations. However, they will need more support, guidance and encouragement; from each other, as we are doing here at this conference; from their professional association, one of which, the Association of College and Research Libraries, has recently revised and published its "Guidelines for Extended Campus Library Services" (ACRL, 1982); and from their own institutions, who in seeking accreditation or reaccreditation for their colleges and universities must respond to the standards of their own regional accreditation association. If that association is moot on the topic, guidance for developing and responsibility for supporting the operation and maintenance of those services is missing at a critical level in the educational process. I would encourage academic librarians to seek out their respective regional accreditation officials, especially in those regions where off-campus library services are not addressed in the standards, to promote the importance of these special services for accreditation and to request their inclusion in the standards when they are next revised.

Addendum: 1990 Update

Since 1982, the year in which the original research on this project was completed, six of the seven commissions on higher education of the regional accreditation associations have revised their academic library standards. This follow-up study, which again reviewed all of the commissions' current academic library standards statements, was conducted to determine what change, if any, had occurred regarding regional accreditation requirements for off-campus library services.

In 1982, only two of the seven commissions on higher education included requirements for the academic library to provide off-campus library services in those instances where off-campus academic programs existed. By 1990, five commissions make specific reference to the need to do so -- an increase of over forty percent. Significant progress indeed!

Two commissions remain without off-campus library services requirements for accreditation: the New England Association and the North Central Association. However, as in 1982, neither is entirely moot on the general topic. They still refer to the concept implicitly by suggesting that the academic library establish cooperative arrangements with other libraries to supplement or exchange resources or services where the need to do so is indicated.

The New England Association has, in fact, not revised its academic library standards since 1980, so there actually hasn't been any opportunity for a change to have occurred. It is, however, in the process of revising all of its standards, including those for the library, at this time. On the other hand, the North Central Association (1988, 1990-92) has totally revised its institutional standards in scope and format since 1982, but it still makes no reference to off-campus library services specifically.

The original three commissions with existing standards on off-campus library services in 1982 have all revised their standards documents, but only one revision resulted in any change to the 1982 off-campus library services standard. The standards of the Northwest Association (1988) and the Commission for Community and Junior College of the Western Association (1987) have remained virtually the same. The Commission for Community and Junior Colleges is planning yet another revision of its standards in 1990, but again doesn't anticipate any changes. However, standard 5 (now standard 6.B.2) for the Commission for Senior Colleges and Universities of the Western Association was changed in 1988 from this more general reference to off-campus library services, "Library and learning resources are readily available and used by the institution's academic community, both on and off campus," (p. 28) to this more expanded version,

> The institution provides services and holds readily available basic collection at all program sites not serviced by the main library. Interlibrary loan or contractual use arrangements may be used to

supplement basic holdings, but are not used as the main
source of learning resources. (p. 62)

The two commissions which, since 1982, have added academic library
standards specifically requiring off-campus library services are the
Southern Association and the Middle States Association. The 1988
revision of the Middle States Association's *Characteristics of Excellence*
added the following specific wording regarding off-campus library
services: "Multi-campus institutions and those with off-campus
programs should design special procedures systems to provide sufficient
on-site access to learning resources." (p. 16)

The Southern Association actually did have an off-campus library
services standard available for review in 1983; but it was then only a
proposed revision and, therefore, not included in the original tally of
higher education commissions with off-campus statements. It was
published at that time in *College and Research Library News*, (1983) to
seek review and comment by librarians in the region as well as
librarians in the field. In the commission' final standard document,
published a year later, this new section was highlighted with its own
heading "Library Resources at Off-Campus Sites," and is included in its
entirety below:

> At any off-campus location where credit courses are
> offered, an institution must ensure the provision of an
> access to adequate learning resources and services
> required to support the courses, programs and degrees
> offered. The institution must own the learning resources
> or provide them through formal arrangements.
>
> Competent library personnel must be assigned duties in
> planning and providing library resources and services
> and in ascertaining their continued adequacy.
>
> When formal arrangements are established for the
> provision of library resources and services, they must
> ensure access to library resources pertinent to the
> programs offered by the institution and must include
> provision for services and resources which support the
> institution's specific programs, the field of study and at
> the degree level offered. (p. 32)

The Southern Association's standard could well serve as a model statement for other regional accreditation commissions to consider for future revisions of their standards. That standards identifying the need for off-campus services for regional accreditation purposes have been added by two more commissions since 1982 is an indication of the continuing importance of library services to the students enrolled in those off-campus programs.

References

Association of College and Research Libraries. Standards and Accreditation Committee. (1982). Guidelines for extended campus library services. *College and Research Libraries News*, *43*, 86-88.

DuMont, R.R. (1980). A conceptual basis for library effectiveness. *College and Research Libraries*, *41*, 103-11.

Holley, E.G. (1983). New accreditation criteria proposed. *College and Research Library News*, *44*, 71-74.

Kania-Schicchi, A. (1984). *The development of a model set of regional accreditation standards for academic libraries.* Unpublished doctoral dissertation, Rutgers University.

Middle States Association of Colleges and Schools. Commission on Higher Education. (1982). *Characteristics of excellence in higher education: Standards for accreditation.* Philadelphia: Middle States Association.

Middle States Association of Colleges and Schools. Commission on Higher Education. (1988). *Characteristics of excellence in higher education: Standards for accreditation.* Philadelphia: Middle States Association.

New England Association of Schools and Colleges. Commission on Institutions of Higher Education. (1980). *Criteria for candidacy and accreditation.* Winchester, MA: New England Association.

New England Association of Schools and Colleges. Commission on Institutions of Higher Education. (1980). *A guide to the process of self-evaluation: Policies and procedures.* Worcester, MA: New England Association.

North Central Association of Colleges and Schools. Commission on Institutions of Higher Education. (1988). *The combined data and evaluation form.* Chicago: North Central Association.

North Central Association of Colleges and Schools. Commission on Institutions of Higher Education. (1982). *Handbook of accreditation.* Chicago: North Central Association.

North Central Association of Colleges and Schools. Commission on Institutions of Higher Education. (1990-92). *A handbook of accreditation.* Chicago: North Central Association.

Northwest Association of Schools and Colleges. Commissions on Colleges. (1984). *Accreditation standards.* Seattle: Northwest Association.

Northwest Association of Schools and Colleges. Commissions on Colleges. (1988). *Standards.* Seattle: Northwest Association.

Western Association of Schools and Colleges. Accrediting Commission for Community and Junior Colleges. (1978). *Handbook of accreditation.* Aptos, CA: Western Association.

Western Association of Schools and Colleges. Accrediting Commission for Community and Junior Colleges. (1987). *Handbook of accreditation.* Aptos, CA: Western Association.

Western Association of Schools and Colleges. Accrediting Commission for Senior Colleges and Universities. (1979). *Handbook of accreditation.* Oakland, CA: Western Association.

Western Association of Schools and Colleges. Accrediting Commission for Senior Colleges and Universities. (1988). *Handbook of accreditation.* Oakland, CA: Western Association.

Note

[1] Dr. Kania's paper was presented at the second Off-campus Library Services Conference, Knoxville, Tennessee, and appeared in the 1986 edition of the conference proceedings.

An Accreditor's Perspective on Off-campus Library Programs[1]

Terrence J. MacTaggart

Introduction

The rather dun colored title of this presentation, "An Accreditor's Perspective on Off-campus Library Program," might be improved with this addition: "Or How To Bring About A Renaissance In Nontraditional Learning: The Librarian's Role." I suggest this more grandiose title because I think the nontraditional movement in higher education is at a critical juncture in its history. It has reached a turning point. The movement will either maintain its creative, innovative and flexible response to the legitimate learning needs of adults or it will become increasingly stratified, rigid and less responsive to the unique styles and preferences of adult learners. I think that librarians and learning resource specialists can play a pivotal role in bringing about a renaissance in adult education, a renaissance characterized by renewed vitality and higher standards of quality than we have witnessed in the past.

Allow me to clarify my role as an accreditor. I am not an official representative of the North Central Association where I do most of my consultant-evaluator work or any other accrediting agency or COPA - The Council on Post-Secondary Accreditation. From that point of view I am without portfolio. Nevertheless, for the past ten years I have served as a consultant evaluator, initially with the Northwest Association of Schools and Colleges and for the past several years with the North Central Association.   In particular, several of my assignments have been to examine nontraditional institutions. And on teams that address fairly traditional institutions, I am the fellow who is often asked to look at the off-campus program, or the continuing education activity, or their assessment of prior experiential learning. Thus, in the course of these ten years I have had an opportunity to examine the range of offerings of off-campus library services in support of these new programs.

My comments readily fall under three headings. What is the role of the accrediting agency, particularly with respect to off-campus library services? Number two, as an accreditor, what am I content to observe in off-campus library offerings? What is the current state of the art? What is an acceptable level of performance? And thirdly, what would make this accreditor jump for joy in an off-campus learning resource setting? The answer to that third question constitutes the renaissance I mentioned a few moments ago.

Role of Accreditation

What is the role of the accrediting body? Essentially, accreditors have two functions. The first is to ensure the public that good service is being offered in exchange for the public reliance on and frequently public payment for that service. This is the evaluative function of accrediting bodies or, if you will, the certifying function. The second major role is to help institutions to improve themselves, through self-evaluation, through external review by the accrediting body and a report, and through actions that may be taken based on those evaluations. This is the consultative role of accrediting bodies.

Accrediting bodies are conservative agencies. Very frequently, they lag behind innovations in the field. Thus, some accrediting bodies are now referring explicitly to standards for assessing experiential learning which developed some years ago by CAEL, the Council for the Advancement of Experiential Learning. I think most of us would agree that it is a good thing that accrediting agencies remain modest in their statements because of their immense power to modify institutional behavior. It is best that this power be wielded very carefully.

I hope I do not sound like a critic of accrediting agencies because I certainly am not. I believe that they are one of the wonders of American higher education, and this is so largely because of their self-restraint and because of what they have prevented others from achieving. For example, accrediting bodies could easily have become a kind of medieval guild which would restrict entry of new providers and limit innovations. But, from my experience, they have been rather open to change and open to new ways of evaluating nontraditional programs. Some of their critics, in fact, allege that they have been too liberal in recognizing alternative ways of serving new populations.

Secondly, had it not been for the operations of accrediting bodies, we could easily have found ourselves victims of a national "ministry of education." By acting as kind of a buffer state between the autocratic impulses of the central government, be it state or federal, and the libertarian impulses of individuals schools, accrediting agencies have helped us to preserve a high degree of institutional autonomy.

The conclusion of all this is that we should not look, by and large, to accrediting agencies for leadership or innovation in educational practice. In fact, we prefer that they do not exercise that kind of action. Instead, they provide minimalist standards.

Off-Campus Library Services

What do accrediting agencies have to say about library services in off-campus settings? Quite simply, the answer is not much.

I have reviewed the accreditation handbooks, policy manuals, and special statements on off-campus programs and library resources issued by the major regional accrediting bodies. The following statements from the Accrediting Commission for Community and Junior Colleges of the Western Association (WASC) are more extensive than some but fairly typical. Its Standard No. 6 on learning resources says, for example, that learning resources ought to be "suited to a variety of student needs and learning styles," that holdings should be "sufficient in quantity and quality to meet the needs of students and the objectives of the institution," that holdings should be "balanced in direct relationship to the nature and level of curricular offerings," and that resources should be "adequately supported in relationship to the total budget." In instances where off-campus programs rely on libraries other than those of the sponsoring institution, this WASC guideline calls for explicit agreements with that cooperating library. The accrediting agencies use similarly general terms -- adequate, sufficient, suitable, balanced -- to describe standards for off-campus library services. The most proscriptive terminology lies in Standard 6 of the Accrediting Commission for Senior Colleges and Universities of WASC. Its infamous standard 6.B.2 reads that "the institution provides services and holds readily available basic collections at all program sites not serviced by the main library. Interlibrary loan or contractual use arrangements may be used to supplement basic holdings, but are not used as the main source of learning resources." The Western Association does not introduce any rationale that I am aware of as to why these cooperative arrangements, loan arrangements and so on, if they are adequate to the task, cannot be the "main" source of materials. Aside from general statements, other accrediting bodies have been content to leave judgement of the adequacy of library resources up to the institutions and individual accrediting teams.

Clearly, if we rely on the announcements of accrediting agencies alike, we will not find much specific direction for the quality of off-campus library services.

Adequate Services

What satisfies me as an accreditor when I examine an off-campus program? In responding to this, I must say I am indebted to the many earlier presentations offered at these conferences. The components of an adequate library support system for off-campus programs would include:

1. Where practicable, an agreement with local municipal, military, college, or university libraries for students and faculty use. These cooperating libraries need to have collections that are relevant to the curriculum being offered. The Off-campus program needs to have meaningful input into acquisition decisions of the cooperating library. Ideally, the agreement would be one which would help ensure a long-term relationship between the cooperating libraries. This is not a heady set of demands, but the sponsoring institution should be willing to pay for the services provided by the cooperating library.

2. In most instances there should also be a site-based collection of library and learning resources. At the very least these would include basic references suitable to the curriculum. The site should also provide the capacity for data base searches.

3. There should be an efficient, timely and free retrieval service which would allow learning resources to be sent from the main campus to the off-campus location. This implies, of course, that the main campus has developed multiple copies of sufficient resources so they can meet demand from different sites at the same time. I must say that Central Michigan University is to be complimented on its leadership in establishing a first-rate system of access to library materials.

4. The fourth characteristic of adequate support is the availability of trained staff on site. If the site is large enough, then it should be able to support a full-time librarian. Otherwise, a circuit rider approach may be necessary in which that librarian is available on a scheduled basis.

5. The fifth feature of strong off-campus programs is evidence of active involvement by the library with faculty, staff and students to ensure that all groups are knowledgeable of the resources available through the learning resource center. Guest lectures, special workshops, and publications which call attention to learning resources are all necessary.

6. There should be evidence of a close link with the curriculum being offered. This is a manageable task, particularly because so many off-campus programs have a specialized curriculum.

Development of Off-Campus Services

If these features would satisfy an accreditor, what would really ring his bell? Before responding to that question, let me put the development of off-campus library services into a developmental context. Based on my experience with these sorts of programs over the last twenty years, I can envision three phases in their development.

The first is the primitive or, to use our historical analogy, the Dark Ages of off-campus library services. Off-campus academic programs at this stage were developing so fast that there scarcely seemed time to build the learning resource infra-structure. There was such competition, particularly in the military base offerings, that harried administrators were more anxious to open up new sites than to build quality programs at existing ones. Reproducing a comprehensive array of library services at off-campus sites seemed impossible. What resources were provided were frequently irrelevant or inadequate. I know of one institution, for example, that began by sending five books per course to each off-campus site. It could hardly be regarded as a library resource but rather as a set of "outside readings."

When access to local libraries was provided, it was very often not by specific written agreement but merely available to the students in the program as it might be to any citizen in the region. Moreover, access to a municipal library in a small town or an on-base military library was frequently a wholly inadequate substitute for a comprehensive academic library. In these early dark days, "loan" services were often so slow that the books arrived well after the course had been completed. In some instances, where the will to provide adequate resources was present, knowledge of the way to do so was not. Particularly if off-campus programs that had highly student-directed courses of study, program managers were uncertain as to what appropriate library resources would be.

Fortunately we are beyond the Dark Ages in this arena and any institution which supports an off-campus program with such minimal resources would be wholly unacceptable today.

The current phase, which I would call the Late Medieval Period (which was actually a time of economic prosperity and relatively high cultural and intellectual achievement) is one characterized by appropriate agreements, local resources based at the site as well as an efficient retrieval system, along with the other characteristics that I mentioned earlier. Some institutions like Central Michigan, have achieved this standard while others have yet to implement it fully.

Renaissance in Off-Campus Library Services

What is the next stage? What is the Renaissance that I referred to earlier? Essentially, it involves not so much the addition of more resources at the site but a radically altered role for the librarian. It involves a movement of librarians and library resources from a supporting role to the center-stage role in these adult learning programs.

Why should this come about? This reason, I think, it that there is a widening gap between the theory of adult learning and its actual practice, and librarians are uniquely positioned to fill this gap. The theory is familiar. It is characterized by numerous slogans pointing to fairly verifiable reality. We are told that adults are particularly highly motivated, that they prefer courses of study which allow them to exercise self-direction, that they recognize the world around them as a learning resource to a much greater extent than younger students, that they are in fact competent learners already although perhaps not yet competent in the academic sense of that term. I think that all of these characteristics are included in the concept of life-long learning. But, are these features reflected in off-campus programs? My sense is that we are seeing more stratified, rigid degree programs in which, in fact, fewer choices are available to students. In part, this may be due to pressures from some accrediting agencies which, as I suggested earlier, are conservative bodies better prepared to evaluate traditional forms of instruction than nontraditional ones. I think institutions have turned to more traditional off-campus programs because they are comfortable and familiar and because very frequently they can be delivered in more cost-effective ways than the individualized approaches. If this trend continues, we will have gained a kind of standardized quality at the sacrifice of creativity and innovation which sparked nontraditional programs in the early days.

I think some of that creativity, some of that wonder in learning experienced by adults, can return if librarians take a more assertive and even aggressive stance in the development of these off-campus programs. To do so, librarians must transcend their sometimes passive role as "providing support systems" for the faculty and assert themselves as full-fledged members of the educational team. In an information society, it is more important than ever that our students, particularly adult students, become adept at accessing new worlds of information. Faculty plays a critical role in this, but I think librarians can play an even more critical role in linking learners with the vast and dynamic world of information which surrounds them.

How is this to be done? The answer is partly political and partly pedological. On the political side, I think librarians need to work effectively with administrators, faculty leaders and other decision makers in presenting themselves as active agents in the learning process. I think they also need to work carefully with individual faculty members as equals in the production of learning.

On the pedagogical side, I recommend a number of steps:

1) That librarians join with instructors, and this is maybe particularly feasible with new and adjunct professors, as a team in the learning process.

2) That librarians become involved during the course design phase rather than as an adjunct at a later time.

3) That librarians encourage faculty to assign students exploratory research rather than simply outside readings.

4) That the outcomes of the exploratory research be a description of the process in which the students uncovered heretofore hidden information.

5) That emphasis be placed on using the new technologies,

particularly those which are called data-base searches, so that all students have first-hand experience with this intellectual process.

6) That students be asked not only to identify but to become versed in the specialized libraries which affect their disciplines, law libraries, medical libraries, and so on.

7) That more independent studies be centered around identifying and using exotic learning resources, that a focus be given to the process of acquiring information as opposed to summarization, and that librarians be active in managing these independent studies.

8) That as a component of internships, students be required to be familiar with the key research materials that support the field in which they are interning. These might include state statues, federal publications, administrative law publications, industry publications, and so on.

9) And finally, that capstone courses would require close work with the librarian on the research pertinent to the field. The objective is that students would be able to access themselves to state-of-the-art information regarding their area of study and become aware of new trends and cutting edge issues in the field.

These are merely examples of ways in which librarians can become more effective. This initiative would not only inspire accreditors, it would help bring about a renaissance in nontraditional education.

Note

[1] Dr. MacTaggart's paper was presented at the fourth Off-campus Library Services Conference, Charleston, South Carolina, and appeared in the 1989 edition of the conference proceedings.

The Impact on the Extended Campus of State Licensure and Accreditation Regulations Governing Off-campus Library Programs: The Connecticut Experience[1]

William Aguilar and Marie Kascus

Overview

The Board of Governors for Higher Education for the state of Connecticut has recently modified the rules and some regulations which govern off-campus library programs. Some of these regulations are even more specific than the guidelines established by the Association of College and Research Libraries. The revised regulations have had a definite impact on two existing off-campus programs, and they are expected to influence other programs as they come up for licensure and accreditation. In effect, the revised regulations have the potential to improve some programs, but they also have the potential to put some institutions out of the off-campus business.

The paper relates Connecticut's higher education enrollment trends as background information; compares the 1974 and revised 1986 state regulations for licensure and accreditation; and discusses the extent of the problem in terms of the number of in-state and out-of-state programs that could be impacted, the possible reasons institutions may offer for non-compliance with the regulations, and the actual impact of the regulations on two institutions with Connecticut-licensed programs.

Connecticut's Higher Education Enrollment Trends

Connecticut is a relatively small but highly complex state offering its citizenry educational diversity at all levels and in virtually all disciplines. Statistics as of July 31, 1984 indicate that 1,739 accredited programs are available in Connecticut institutions of higher education. An additional thirty-five programs are licensed and eligible for consideration for accreditation, and of these programs, five are offered by out-of-state institutions.

Some of the highlights in Connecticut's enrollment trends are: a total enrollment in 1985 of 160,148 which is a 3% decline from the peak year of 1983 for public institutions, and a 4% deterioration for private institutions; a projected 8% drop for the 1990's, and a projected drop of about 14% between 1985 and 2000; a continued decrease in the full-time student population; a student population in which women constitute the majority and account for the largest proportion of the over twenty-five student population, and a minority population that accounts for 8.1% of the total enrollment.

Of particular concern to Connecticut institutions offering off-campus programs is the fact that New England public institutions experienced a 9% decrease in full-time student enrollment in the fall of 1985 and a 4% increase in part-time enrollment.

There is a growing awareness of the significance of the changes in enrollment patterns and the need to consider these changes in making policy decisions regarding support services, scheduling adjustments and course offerings.

The Board of Governors for Higher Education has recently drafted a strategic plan for Connecticut higher education which uses the changes in enrollment patterns as a springboard for its planning assumptions and makes recommendations that both recognize and address the needs of the off-campus population.

Comparison of the 1974 and 1986 Regulations

By statue the authority to establish regulations concerning the requirements for licensure and accreditation rests with the Board of Governors. Among its provisions, the statue specifically authorizes the Board to establish regulations pertinent to libraries. Section 10a-34 (d) states that "no person, school, board, association or corporation shall operate a program or institutions of higher learning unless it has been licensed or accredited by the Board of Governors." It further states that the Board may accept regional or national accreditation as evidence that a given institution has satisfied the requirements established by the Board.

A comparison of the 1974 regulations with the revised 1986 regulations is reflective of change in focus. Section 10330-16 of the 1974 "Regulations for Licensure and Accreditation" addresses the requirements pertinent to resource centers and libraries. The regulations relate to the adequacy of resources; the need for

procedures to encourage students to use the library; the need for
personnel with appropriate training; the involvement of faculty in the
selection process; and the provision of adequate budgetary support.
the 1974 regulations do not specifically address library support for off-
campus programs. One could assume that the regulations apply
equally to all programs whether on-campus or off-campus.

By comparison, Section 10a-34-18 (d) of the 1986 "Regulations for
Licensure and Accreditation of Institutions and Programs of Higher
Learning" specifically delineate the library support requirements for
off-campus programs. They read as follows:

Section 10a-34-18 *Library and Learning Resources. (d) Off-campus
Programs.* Library support for off-campus programs is subject to
the following requirements:

(1) There shall be provision for a core collection, including
both circulating and reference materials, sufficient to meet the
needs of both students and faculty to be provided either at the
site or via written agreement with a nearby library.

(2) There shall be provision for a reserve reading collection
at or near the site.

(3) There shall be provision professional library staff support
for library services at or near the off-campus site.

(4) There shall be provision for additional materials to
supplement the core collection, e.g., through computerized
bibliographic access and a document delivery system.

(5) There shall be provision for adequate annual budget support
for library resources at or near the site.

To those institutions offering off-campus programs in Connecticut, the
regulations provide a choice of two options: (1) to establish libraries
at the off-campus site or (2) to contract resources, facilities and
services to an area library in close geographic proximity to the program
site. While not explicitly stated in the regulations, experience has
indicated that contractual agreements with area libraries are an
acceptable option only if it can be demonstrated that the contractual
library is prepared to offer resources and services that support the

academic program and are comparable to those available at the home library. A further unstated expectation is that an academic institution will demonstrate the adequacy of the resources of the proposed contract library by faculty evaluation before entering into a contract. Financial reimbursement to the contract library for services rendered would further enhance the contract arrangement as a means of providing library support to the off-campus program.

The revision is a significant one for institutions offering off-campus programs. The question which could be asked is, "Why the revision?" What was the rationale and impetus for the Board's change? One has to assume that the Board of Governors would not adopt new regulations without good cause and after considerable deliberation. Three possible reasons for the Board's initiative are suggested: (1) The Board determined that library support for existing off-campus programs was inadequate. (2) The Board felt the need to strengthen the regulations to insure that support and not lip service was provided. (3) The Board may not have been entirely satisfied with the efforts of regional and national accrediting associations in the area of off-campus programs.

Suggested reasons (1) and (2) are based on subjective interpretation, but (3) warrants further consideration. The 1974 regulations state that the Board could elect to accept the report of a regional accreditation team as evidence that an educational institution was meeting the needs of its students. In the case of one Connecticut institution, a satisfactory accreditation report from the regional accrediting association was not sufficient to insure re-accreditation in the view of the Connecticut Department of Higher Education. The institution in question was directed to address the problem of library services to its off- campus sites in order to comply with the new state regulations. A satisfactory review by a regional association in and of itself is not a guarantee that an academic institution has satisfied the Connecticut regulations for library support to off-campus students.

At issue here is the apparent lack of uniformity among the various accrediting associations in terms of the language of the regulations and the application of the standards to program evaluation. The available literature on regional accrediting associations is not encouraging. In her analysis of regional accreditation standards and off-campus library services, Kania concludes that there is no consistency among the regional accreditation standards as they relate to academic libraries.

She goes on to encourage academic librarians to seek out their respective regional accreditation officials to request the inclusion of off-campus library services in upcoming revisions (p. 145).

The inconsistency in the regulations of the various accrediting associations complicates an already difficult process of fairly assessing non-traditional off-campus programs while not inhibiting program innovation. The report on Missouri's state level effort to review its external degree programs was titled, "Magic or Method," (Lynd, 1981) a title that is reflective of the complexity of the problem and yet the persistent need to undertake such a review to establish criteria that will support quality assurance in academic programs regardless of their point of origin.

The ACRL Guidelines for Extended Library Services are of limited value. Their status as guidelines and not standards diminishes their effectiveness. They provide a signal in the right direction, but they too reflect a similar lack of consensus in the library world as to what level of library support is needed for off-campus programs. In light of the projected enrollment trends and the proliferation of off-campus instructional programs, ACRL may want to modify and upgrade the current guidelines to the level of standards. Upgrading them would reinforce the importance of library services whether on-campus or off-campus.

The Connecticut Board of Governors is moving beyond regional accrediting standards and available professional guidelines for off-campus library support in its commitment to quality assurance for all higher education programs. The Connecticut regulations recognize the importance of library support to the off-campus program and will require academic institutions to go beyond mere rhetoric in complying with the regulations.

In-State and Out-of-State Programs That Could Be Impacted

The Connecticut Department of Higher Education has recently defined an off-campus program to mean any program in which students may complete more than fifty percent of the requirements for a degree at a location other than the primary campus or institution offering the program.

Higher education programs are currently offered at 110 Connecticut sites, forty-eight represent permanent colleges and university facilities. Thus over half of all sites offering higher education programs are subject to the regulations governing off-campus programs.

Six of the sites represent Connecticut licensed programs offered by out-of-state institutions. The regulations make no distinction as to the point of origin of a given academic program. In fact, the regulations are specific and apply equally to in-state and out-of-state institutions. The regulations read as follows:

> Section 10a-34-24 *Programs Offered by Out-of-State Institutions*. (b) *Licensure requirements.* The institution shall be required to demonstrate compliance with all standards in Section 10a-34-24, inclusive of those regulations as they apply to the program(s) to be offered in Connecticut. In addition there shall be qualified on-site administrative staff responsible for the overall administrative operation of all educational activities to include instruction, counseling, advising, library services and maintenance of academic records.

This provision in the regulations regarding out-of-state programs reinforces the state's interest in providing quality assurance for all Connecticut educational programs.

Reasons Institutions May Offer for Non-compliance

It is possible that some institutions with off-campus programs may not be prepared to commit themselves to full acceptance of the new regulations. For some, the concern may be more philosophical and may reflect the fact that they are not convinced of the existence of a problem related to off-campus library support. For others, compliance may be seen as an unnecessary financial burden. Some institutions may even argue that the maturity, independence and motivation of off-campus students precludes the need for special library arrangements for this group. No matter how convincing the responsibility to provide resources or access to resources for all students. Perhaps what is needed is a consciousness-raising campaign to remind institutions of the importance of the library to the total instructional programs and the institution's obligation to provide equally for all of its students. If instructional programs can be offered at a distance, then the services needed to support these programs should be provided.

Academic institutions have been slow in assessing the needs of off-campus students. Off-campus students have been expected to assume a larger burden of responsibility in accessing library resources and services needed to support their course work. These students pay the same tuition and have a right to expect the same services.

Impact of the Regulations on Two Institutions

One way of attempting to assess the potential impact of the regulations is to briefly discuss the experiences of two regulations is to briefly discuss the experiences of two institutions. The first is an in-state institution and is referred to as Institution A. The second is an out-of-state institution and is referred to as Institution B.

Institution A is a relatively small, independent, four year college offering off-campus programs at ten different sites. Half of the sites are open to the public and the other half are only open to a restricted population, e.g., employees of a major corporation. Approximately one third of the students of this college are enrolled in off-campus programs. These students can earn a baccalaureate degree through the institution without having to spend any time at the main campus.

In attempting to meet the library needs of its off-campus students, Institution A has historically relied very heavily on agreements with public libraries. The language of these agreements is very informal and not reflective of any serious commitment or stated expectations. It should be pointed out that this institution has had difficulty in getting academic libraries to enter into contractual agreements.

When faced with the prospect of a moratorium on the establishment of additional program sites and non-licensure, Institution A developed a three-part model for the delivery of library services. In the model, the home library serves as the primary source of materials, an off-campus librarian serves as the primary means of access and delivery, and agreements with selective non-affiliated libraries serve as an enhancement of library services at specific sites. The model provides access to resources, facilities, services and professional staff and thus satisfies the fundamental requirements established by the Board of Governors.

Institution B is a midwestern university with a large number of off-campus programs located throughout the country. Full-time faculty from this institution commute to Connecticut on a weekly basis to provide instruction. Problems resulted in the re-accreditation process because of the new regulations. The major problem for this out-of-state institution was that it could not justify the establishment of a branch library at the Connecticut site. The Institution was also unsuccessful in locating an area library willing to provide services on a contractual basis to its students. Although materials were routinely available at the site, the quantity was deemed to be inadequate to support the curriculum. Moreover, students lacked access to bibliographic tools which would aid them in requesting items directly from the main campus library.

In the case of Institution B, the recommendation made by a site review committee was not to renew licensure of the program. The recommendation was supported by the Department of Higher Education and forwarded to the Board of Governors. The final chapter has yet to be written as Institution B was seeking legal counsel in this matter.

Compliance with the regulations places a greater burden on institutions which do not permanently reside in Connecticut. Existing models for packaging and delivering library services, e.g., contracting for library services or trunk delivery, may not effectively solve the problems faced by out-of-state institutions with programs licensed in Connecticut. These institutions may have to modify existing models for delivery library services at a distance or develop a new model that assures compliance with the revised regulations. For Connecticut libraries, reciprocity is less of an incentive for resource sharing when the institution offering the instructional program is geographically distant from the library with which it seeks a contractual agreement.

Some out-of-state institutions may conclude that the expense of doing business in Connecticut is too high. As a result, they may withdraw their programs. This raises the issue of the possible repercussions on the students matriculated in out-of-state programs. This is especially true if the out-of-state program is unique and in-state institutions are unwilling or unable to offer a comparable program.

Concluding Remarks

The steady decrease in the traditional, full-time student population combined with a steady increase in the non-traditional, part-time student population magnifies the importance of the off-campus program in the overall planning process for higher education in Connecticut. Policy decisions will have to take into consideration the evolving needs of this growing population of students. The evidence suggests that Connecticut is willing to creatively meet the challenge posed by off-campus programs.

The initiative taken by the Board of Governors for Higher Education to strengthen the regulations for licensure and accreditation as they apply to off-campus programs provides leadership in the right direction. It is clear that the new regulations have great potential for improving library services to off-campus students. What is not clear, however, is the full impact that these regulations will have on the state's academic programs. The two institutions discussed provide some insight into the impact of these regulations on the extended campus. More time will be needed to assess the full impact of these regulations.

The message from Connecticut is clear. Off-campus instructional programs must include a provision for library support as an integral component of the program design. Connecticut librarians have an opportunity to assume a leadership role in making certain that library services are a vital aspect of the total educational process, and they will certainly want to capitalize on this opportunity.

References

Association of College and Research Libraries. Standards and Accreditation Committee. (1986). Guidelines for extended campus library services. *College and Research Libraries News, 47*, 189-200.

Kania, T. (1986). Regional accreditation standards and off-campus library service. In Barton M. Lessin (Ed.), *The Off-campus Services Conference Proceedings* (pp. 140-146). Mt. Pleasant, MI: Central Michigan University Press.

Ludwig, M. and Latouf, G. (1986). *Public four-year colleges and universities: A healthy enrollment environment?* Washington, DC:

Office of Communications Services. National Association of State Universities and Land Grant Colleges.

Lynd, A. (1981). Magic or method: Procedures for a state-level review of external degrees. *Conference on Issues in External Degree Programs: The Role of Faculty in Maintaining Quality* (pp. 247--258). Washington, DC: American Council on Education.

New England Association of Colleges and Schools. Commission on the Institutions of Higher Education. (1983). *Accreditation handbook.* Winchester, MA: New England Association.

State of Connecticut. Board of Governors for Higher Education. (1985). *Academic program trends in Connecticut higher education 1979-1984.* Research Report R-2-85.

State of Connecticut. Board of Governors for Higher Education. (1986). *Enrollment trends in Connecticut higher education 1960-1985.* Research Report R-2-86.

State of Connecticut. Board of Governors for Higher Education. (1986). *Investing in Connecticut's future: A strategic plan for higher education.*

State of Connecticut. Board of Governors for Higher Education. (1974). *Regulations for licensure and accreditation.*

State of Connecticut. Board of Governors for Higher Education. (1986). *Regulations for licensure and accreditation of institutions and programs of higher learning.*

Note

[1] The paper prepared by William Aguilar and Marie Kascus was presented at the third Off-campus library Services Conference, Reno, Nevada, and appeared in the 1987 edition of the conference proceedings.

Library Privileges For Off-campus Faculty and Students: The View From An Impacted Library[1]

Patricia M. Kelley

Introduction

Lured by internships, fieldwork, and employment opportunities, students and faculty members who are normally on campus often find themselves far from their home campuses and wanting to use university library collections and services. At the same time, university libraries which are heavily used by these visiting researchers are becoming increasingly reluctant to provide them with free services or free on-site use or library access of any kind. The academic libraries in the Washington, D.C., metropolitan area traditionally have maintained policies of free on-site use of collections and assistance at service desks and have selectively granted borrowing privileges. However, the increase in library use by their own university communities and the dramatically increased use of their libraries by unaffiliated individuals in recent years have created serious dilemmas regarding effective allocation of resources--collections, space, and service staff.

One noticeable group of affiliated users is the off-campus population composed of faculty members who are on leave from their home universities, graduate students who are working on their theses and dissertations, and both undergraduate and graduate students who are engaged in internships, independent study or fieldwork in the Washington Area. They interest me greatly and are the subject of this paper because there is such a heavy concentration of them in the Washington area, where many request library privileges in the Gelman Library at George Washington University and in other libraries of the Consortium of Universities of the Washington Metropolitan Area (hereafter simply called the Consortium). I have spent considerable time over the past twenty months trying to define fair and workable policies regarding their use of the Gelman Library.

Local Situation

The situation at GWU is fairly typical of Consortium institutions. However, the proximity of Gelman Library to federal office buildings and the offices of consulting and research firms and its easy access via public transportation cause it to be one of the most heavily used by unaffiliated researchers. Although GWU is a private university, most of its collections are available for in-house use by anyone who can produce a current photo-identification card and sign his/her name on the register at the front door. Our entrance statistics indicate that approximately one out of every ten people who walk through the front door is not affiliated with GWU. We are considering restricting reference assistance and already limit the use of some collections to students at GWU and other Consortium universities. Unless demands for service stop growing, we will probably increase the restrictions on non-GWU (that is, non-Consortium) library users. I estimate that we currently turn away twenty requesters for every person who is granted borrowing privileges.

A noticeable proportion of the non-GWU people who request borrowing privileges or use materials on-site are students at non-Consortium universities. The magnitude of the problem is hidden by the fact that employed students use their employee identification cards to gain entrance to the building, so they appear on our register as employees of firms and government agencies. It may be that as we investigate appropriate fee-based services or other restrictions that would affect firms, we will find that more of those people start to identify themselves as students.

Ours is a true library of the eighties--strongly supporting resource sharing while planning to expand the use of fees as an alternative to either unlimited free service or denial of service to external users. Therefore, it is very important to consider where the needs of unaffiliated off-campus students and faculty who use Gelman as their "away" library fit into our service philosophy.

Most off-campus requesters fit into the following groups, presented here in order of our willingness to provide services. I will explain how we respond to their needs and why.

1. Faculty members on sabbatical

2. Doctoral students writing dissertations

3. Master's candidates writing theses and students engaged in independent study related to our special collections

4. Administrators of off-campus programs who want to negotiate library services for students and faculty enrolled in their programs; and individual faculty members in those programs who have the same purpose

5. Individual interns seeking borrowing privileges; or the library directors, provosts, or program directors who want to arrange for library privileges for their Washington interns

Privileges for Off-campus Faculty

Recognizing that our stated library mission includes service to the broader academic community as well as to the GWU community, we are most receptive to external faculty and graduate students engaged in genuine scholarly research. As a professional courtesy, we are happy to permit faculty members who are on sabbatical to use our collections and borrow circulating materials. Our only requirement is that we receive a letter or phone call from the home library directors verifying university affiliation and status as borrowers-in-good-standing. The library director who denies a professor or student the necessary letter of recommendation is not to be envied. However, because we do not require to the home institution to guarantee payment of fines and replacement of materials, we must ask them to screen out anyone who may cause us problems.

Problems arise in categorizing faculty who are on leave to work in government agencies, international organizations, etc. Some may be on loan, in effect, or have earned an appointment as an academic honor. Others, however, have taken leave to work as consultants, or contracted to conduct research programs and, in our view, should be subject to the same service restrictions and fees as other employees, consultants, and free-lance researchers. Washington is filled with researchers and consultants, many of whom are faculty members either temporarily or sporadically working there. Our difficulty is finding a way to distinguish between off-campus faculty who are in Washington to pursue scholarly research and those who are engaging in free enterprise.

We deny requests for courtesy privileges in cases where we feel that the faculty member is using it for business purposes. As a researcher's use of our library crosses that fuzzy gray line separating scholarly endeavor from business, we become less generous with our collections and staff time. The greatest threat to our liberal policy concerning off-campus faculty is abuse of the privilege. As we impose fees and limit free services to the verification of the faculty requester's research status. Surely, the home library director will not be in a position to provide that verification. But who would be willing to provide that information?

Privileges for Off-campus Doctoral and Masters Candidates

Our liberal policy on borrowing privileges extends to doctoral candidates and is our way of offering them encouragement to our doctoral candidates wherever they have wandered. Some students apply for borrowing privileges or building passes (which simply eases their entrance to the building) because we have strong collections in their fields. In most cases, however, they select Gelman Library because they need an academic library that is conveniently located.

For a short time, we tried to restrict borrowing privileges to students who were working in fields where we felt we had a research level collection. But that required such time-consuming negotiations, not to mention the risk of having some sensitive person at GWU learn about and feel offended by our judgment that a collection in his/her field is not research level, that we quickly abandoned the process. Most important, the practice seemed to be an unnecessary barrier for students who, in most instances, have gone to Washington because they have found jobs there and now carry the burden of working all day and writing a dissertation all night.

Following the same policy we use for faculty, we require a letter from the library director verifying that the applicant is a doctoral candidate and a borrower-in-good-standing. Only students who have reached the dissertation stage of their studies are granted borrowing privileges. On the application form, they sign a statement agreeing to acknowledge their use of the Gelman Library in dissertation research. In that way, the library receives a little public recognition in return. Finally, we supply some incentive for working diligently on the dissertation: free borrowing privileges expire after one year and cannot be renewed. After that time, the student may obtain limited borrowing privileges by joining the Friends of the Libraries and paying a fee.

Students sometimes consider the request for the letter to be a barrier to obtaining borrowing privileges. Some will try to substitute letters from dissertation advisors or general letters of introduction. Both are unacceptable because they fail to answer the crucial question, "Is this person a reliable library user?" The advisor does not have to face our university librarian twice a year at meetings of the American Library Association or may not realize that a bad experience would jeopardize library privileges for other students from that university. The library director, on the other hand, has any number of sound professional reasons for screening unreliable borrower's. At least I hope that's the reason why some students fail to complete the application process. Sometimes there is considerable delay in receipt of letters. On occasion the letter is so insistent that the home library accepts *no* financial responsibility for the student borrowers that I can but wonder if there is a warning being issued.

We receive requests from master's candidates who are doing research for their theses or from students who are engaged in independent study projects. If the student is truly writing a thesis or if the research relates to one of our special collections, and upon receipt of the necessary letter from the home library director, we grant full access and borrowing privileges for one semester. The more typical requester, however, is the student who claims to be working on a thesis or engaged in an internship with a government agency or professional association. It would seem that the word "thesis" can be a generic term used loosely to describe any long research paper or report; and "fieldwork" is research conducted in a new environment. But we have adopted a very firm line in denying borrowing privileges or use of restricted collections unless we are convinced that the student is engaged in scholarly research.

So far, we have had excellent cooperation from the students who have borrowing privileges and only mild protest about our renewal policy. At the first sign of a problem, however, we would notify the home library director and cancel borrowing privileges or, in the case of a general behavioral problem, bar a student from our library. As the lending library, we take all of the risks in granting any privilege because the home university typically accepts no responsibility. If is important for students and faculty to obtain privileges off-campus, perhaps we should reconsider the home institution's responsibilities for the member its librarians and academic department or advisors supply with letters of reference. What should a letter of introduction mean?

Interns as Off-campus Students

Only under the most exceptional circumstances do we grant borrowing privileges to other masters candidates or to undergraduates. We are confident that the demand from interns and non-Consortium off-campus students is far greater than we could handle without detracting from the service our own students have the right to expect in their own library. We have been unsuccessful in devising objective criteria for granting privileges to some, while denying others, and we are unwilling to invest in the time required to negotiate hundreds of individual requests.

Interns, for example, number in the thousands in Washington. There seems to be no estimate in print of the number of internships available in the Washington area; but I can assure you that private firms, government agencies at tall levels, international organizations, and trade and professional associations regularly accept interns. To give some idea of the number, the *Directory of Internships, Work Experience Programs, and on-the-Job Training Opportunities* (1976) and its 1978 supplement together list nearly two hundred organizational sponsors in Washington, not including Maryland and Virginia. Each organization sponsors from a few interns to several hundred each year.

There are two type of internships. The first, usually held by undergraduates, is administered by a college or university. The places students and usually gives course credit for the experience. A program director or librarian from the home institution is likely to try to arrange for borrowing privileges or building passes for the whole group. Based on my conversations with these requesters, however, I find no convincing reason to grant either privilege. It seems that the argument made by the program director is that interns may receive research assignments, so they need to use a library. Moreover, the director feels they may need to feel welcome on a college campus, where they can mix with others their own age in their spare time.

While both concerns seem valid, the second one is not a legitimate library service need. Certainly the Gelman Library has no need to encourage anyone to participate in the social aspects of undergraduate library life. It already has more participants than it needs. While the research assignments certainly will require use of a library, the student will be engaged in research as a staff member in the sponsoring organization and should have the same access to this library as his/her fellow employees. If the purpose of an internship is to gain practical experience in a chosen field, then learning the constraints of the position is a valuable part of the lesson.

The second type of internship, filled by both graduate and undergraduate students who frequently are paid for their work, is individually negotiated by the student. He/she, more obviously than the first intern, is an employee of the agency. He/she is also likely to arrive with a letter of introduction from a reference librarian or faculty advisor and does not give up easily when denied borrowing privileges.

It seems to me that the off-campus status of interns is deserving of some attention within the colleges and universities that sponsor them. If there is a legitimate need for academic library services that is different from their library needs as employees, that should be identified and provided. The two most frequently articulated reasons given by students who want borrowing privileges are: they have term papers to write as a result of their carrying incompletes from the previous semester; and interlibrary loan is not fast enough to serve their purposes. Perhaps students who have incompletes pending should not be eligible for internships. Certainly unwillingness to use the agency's interlibrary loan service is not sufficient reason for us to grant borrowing privileges.

In short, colleges and universities need to define more clearly to students the purpose and conditions of the internship and take the initiative to deny the letter of introduction unless some legitimate reason for a student to use a specific library can be stated in the letter. Hand-carried letters addressed to no specific library, giving no reason for library use, failing to vouch for the student as a library user, and which are sometimes signed by a research assistant or someone else whose position is totally unclear, give the impression that no one at the home institution has taken the time to determine whether or not this intern needs library privileges in an academic library.

"Traditional" Off-campus Students

Finally, although they are outside the main focus of this paper, a little needs to be said about our service to students enrolled in non-Consortium off-campus programs. I would like to explain very briefly why we seldom contract with other universities to provide services even though contractual arrangements would seem to be a practical way of coping with the demand for service by that group. Under very unusual circumstances we do contract for services. Throughout 1984, for example, more than two hundred of these off-campus students were eligible for full-student privileges in Gelman Library under our agreements with three universities. The identity of the individuals changed from semester-to-semester, but the total remained fairly constant. Three-quarters of those eligible actually registered as borrowers. Two universities paid fees which were based on the number of students expected to enroll in the program. On an experimental basis, the third university · gave us some special interlibrary loan privileges in exchange. Although that is not an even exchange by any means, for the present we are willing to make the agreement for political reasons.

While I would be reluctant to enter into service agreements with additional institutions on the same bases as we have with those three, I feel certain we could devise contractual services that would provide for the needs of those off-campus students without creating service delays for our own students and faculty. From a library service perspective, our primary concern about the number of unaffiliated users of our library is that GWU and Consortium students find themselves queuing for reference service and high-demand materials. We have not devised contractual services because that would not be in the best interest of other parts of the university.

Member universities of the Consortium offer extensive evening programs both on and off-campus. There is terrific competition in recruitment of part-time students throughout the Washington Area, which is considered on of the best off-campus markets in the country because of the high concentration of middle and upper level civilian and military government positions. It recent years, the competition has increased significantly as more universities have opened off-campus programs there or expanded programs already in place. Since access to library resources is a prerequisite for state accreditation of most off-campus programs, our contracts to supply library privileges could undermine our own university's competitive edge in this region's off-campus marketplace. Of course, mutual support is the underpinning of a consortium, so we also have to be careful not to undermine our partners' offerings. As a result, we do not enter into agreements with universities which offer off-campus courses that compete with programs offered by any Consortium-member institution.

Recently, state universities in Maryland and Virginia joined the Consortium. Because their public responsibilities may differ from those of the private colleges and universities in the District of Columbia, the whole question of who can be denied privileges probably will have to be addressed through new agreements. Meanwhile, what might be possible or desirable from a purely library service perspective is a moot question. In the absence of defined and enforced limits to access, the academic libraries in the Washington Area remain open for on-site use by off-campus students regardless of their home affiliations.

That on-site use is not satisfactory or sufficient is evident in the barrage of requests for borrowing privileges received at public service desks at the beginning of the semester. Our unverified impression, based on observations of service staff and some evidence from the entrance registry, is that Gelman has a significant population of non-GWU off-campus students. This is not surprising since part-time students are particularly prone to use the most convenient library (Whitlatch, 1981). Convenience is a Gelman Library hallmark.

Conclusion

As we grapple daily with the influx of unaffiliated users, it is easy to begin viewing them as a single "problem" that we could solve by charging discouraging fees or limiting the hours during which they would be permitted to use our libraries. In reality, that group consists of several different types of users, some of whom we feel we have a professional obligation to serve as a means of encouraging reciprocity in resource sharing. After all, our students and faculty use libraries far and wide--if they can get in. There are limits, however, to our ability to provide for so many. Only with the cooperation of other universities will we be able to sort out the needs it is reasonable for us to address from the ones that might better be directed elsewhere. We are sensitive to the needs of off-campus individuals, but the concentration of them in this geographical region makes it impossible for us to serve them all.

References

Directory of Internships, Work Experience Programs, and On-the-Job Training Opportunities. (1976). Thousand Oaks, CA: Ready Reference Press.

1st Supplement to Directory of Internships, Work Experience Programs, and On-the-Job Training Opportunities. (1978). Thousand Oaks, CA: Ready Reference Press.

Whitlatch, Jo Bell. (1981). *San Jose State University Library Services: Results of the spring 1980 Faculty and Student User Surveys*. San Jose, CA: California State University, San Jose. (ERIC Document Reproduction Service No. ED 206-279)

Note

[1] Ms. Kelley's paper was presented at the second Off-campus Library Services Conference, Knoxville, Tennessee, and appeared in the 1986 edition of the conference proceedings.

Faculty Perspectives Regarding Educational Supports In Off-Campus Courses[1]

John E. Cook and Mary Lou Wranesh Cook

Quality in academic programs (courses) is dependent upon a triad of (a) faculty, (b) students, and (c) logistics or course supports. It appears that a significant amount of research has been conducted (formal and especially informal) on the perceptions of students and administrators regarding off-campus courses or programs (Kansas State University, 1984). Students are generally mature, highly motivated, and very enthusiastic regarding such courses or programs. Less research has been conducted as to their academic abilities or qualifications and the impact of those qualifications upon the academic quality of such programs. Still less research has been conducted regarding faculty perspectives regarding off-campus courses and programs (Cook & Cook, 1984, Johnson, 1984). This report focuses upon faculty perspectives regarding off-campus courses and specifically the impact of logistics or course supports upon the perceived quality of such courses.

Faculty are the key to the quality and effectiveness of an academic course or program. They are especially critical off-campus since they in effect become the microcosmic representation of the entire institution for some short period of time. Logistics or course supports have three potential effects upon an academic course. Course supports can enhance the effectiveness of a course, they can be relatively neutral in effect, or they can inhibit learning. The effect may well be directly related to the type of course, to the faculty member, and/or the pedagogy employed. Course supports would fall primarily as hygiene in the Herzberg Hygiene/Motivator Theory Scale (Herzberg, Mausner & Snyderman, 1959). A well-equipped classroom or good parking may not improve learning or enhance student motivation, but a poor classroom or inadequate parking can clearly inhibit learning. Student access to appropriate course supports such as an adequate library, computer facilities, and clinical or practicum facilities are essential to maintain quality in off-campus programs. Support for faculty to have adequate logistics such as audio-visual equipment and materials, secretarial support, and back-up procedures for numerous anomalies is essential. Good supports may not motivate a faculty member to teach better but poor course supports can clearly inhibit the faculty from the best possible performance.

The Survey

Identifying institutions with off-campus programs was difficult. Catalogues generally did not include listings or descriptions of these outreach courses. Often the courses and programs were offered on a one-time basis and were not publicized except at the time and location of the offering. A good census of such institutions did not appear to be available.

Questionnaires were distributed by mail to a primarily convenience sample. In all situations, a director of the program was identified. This person was asked to distribute the questionnaires to faculty. Faculty teaching off-campus courses were identified in a number of ways, including advertisements, conference proceedings, word of mouth, and serendipity. These faculty had a variety of backgrounds and varying lengths of experience in teaching off-campus.

A significant number of responses were received from faculty associated with Chapman College. Questionnaires were distributed to centers operated by Chapman College primarily on military installations. The Chapman administration was very cooperative in requesting the various center directors to distribute the questionnaires to appropriate faculty. This portion of the returns represented a nationwide (with some off-shore responses) sample of opinion. One other institution with multiple centers was identified and solicited but did not respond.

A directory listing all National League for Nursing accredited baccalaureate nursing programs was reviewed and questionnaires were distributed to twenty schools offering part-time programs, with the assumption that some of these would include off-campus courses.

A two-page or sixteen-item questionnaire was developed to identify the faculty perceptions regarding educational course supports when teaching in off-campus credit courses or programs. The questionnaire was designed to be brief, requiring primarily check marks as responses to questions. Comments were requested at the end of the questionnaire. The survey responses were confidential. A postmark on the envelope was the only potential indication of the respondent's identity, unless the survey was voluntarily signed.

Results and Discussion

Basic information was collected: length of time teaching in outreach and primarily full-time position. Faculty perceptions regarding several areas were surveyed: arrangement of course supports, meeting course objectives, and student level of learning. Respondents chose from descriptive choices to classify their perspectives. Business reply envelopes were also included with the questionnaires. Responses were returned directly to the authors. One hundred sixty-eight completed questionnaires were returned in a six-week period.

Two broad categories of faculty were identified as typical instructors in off-campus programs. One category was regular full-time faculty who teach off-campus because they are assigned to do so as a portion of their regular assignment or teach off-campus for extra compensation. A subset of this group was full-time faculty of one institution teaching part-time for a different institution off-campus. These individuals had the choice "academician" to select. The second category of faculty identified as typical for off-campus courses were individuals whose primary job was not teaching but teaching part-time in an off-campus course or program. These individuals had the choice of "practitioner" to select. Most faculty responding did choose between the two on the force-choice basis but a few wrote notes or comments that they considered themselves to be both academicians and practitioners.

Responses were divided almost equally between the two broad categories with 54% choosing "practitioner" and 46% selecting "academician." The sample is somewhat skewed because of the large number of Chapman College faculty responding since most Chapman centers are located too far from the Chapman home campus for full-time faculty to commute. The non-Chapman responses are more skewed to "academician" but that appears to be again a function of the population selected. In reviewing the data we will continue to reflect upon the potential biases of the responses. Based upon observation of several off-campus programs, the mix of "academicians" and "practitioners" appears relatively common for such programs in general.

The time scheduling of off-campus courses would seem to be an important factor in determining the potential quality or effectiveness of such courses or programs. It appears that most off-campus courses are non-traditional in location and also in scheduling. One item was included to elicit faculty perspectives or opinion regarding the scheduling of courses.

The presupposed assumption in the item was that courses off-campus are scheduled primarily for the convenience of students. This seems an obvious assumption since most courses off-campus are there primarily because the students cannot or will not come to campus. The choice "convenience of students" received 63% of the responses. Some faculty selected more than one option. The second most common selection was "availability of facilities" but that selection only received 17% of the responses. These two options accounted for 80% of the responses. The Chapman and non-Chapman responses both reflected approximately an 80% response to these two items with the non-Chapman response being slightly stronger toward "convenience of students."

"Off-campus courses tend to be scheduled most for good educational technique" received an 11% response from both Chapman and non-Chapman returns. This item would appear to be very important since 89% of respondents chose something else. It may partially be explained that some respondents viewed the question as a forced-choice item and they selected only the strongest choice. Other faculty opted for multiple responses. Whatever effect this had, it is clear that most faculty do not perceive the manner of scheduling off-campus courses is based upon good educational technique. Different faculty and different courses require a variety of education techniques that do not always fit the scheduling model found off-campus. More flexibility or creativity in scheduling models ought to be developed.

The least selected faculty perspective is that classes are scheduled for the "convenience of faculty" with a 9% response. The non-Chapman segment reported 8%. Although remarks are generally not included in this report, a significant number of comments were made regarding the difficulty of teaching off-campus. These were most often from faculty traveling to the off-campus location. Since faculty generally perceive that classes are scheduled primarily for the availability of facilities or the convenience of students and not for faculty convenience, attention must be focused upon the resulting faculty morale and the impact upon their teaching effectiveness.

Arrangement of course supports such as library services are a necessity for all academic courses. They may be arranged by a program administrator. Faculty teaching courses inform administrators of the necessary texts, journals, and equipment for the course, and the administrator assumes responsibility for making these available. Faculty may be responsible for making their own arrangements for these supports, and may even request this responsibility. Of our sample 48% reported these arrangements were made by the program administrator. Another 51% of the responding faculty members made their own arrangements. One percent responded that course arrangements were a joint effort between themselves and the program administrator. Many more persons may have believed this was a shared responsibility, but most respondents made a choice from the two alternatives listed on the survey.

This survey made no attempt to discover the adequacy of supports such as physical facilities and audio-visual equipment. It seems of importance to these authors that appropriate course supports be available and accessible for use in each course offered. Obviously courses and professors have different needs, but the flexibility should exist to allow for optimal use of these services when desired by the professor.

Faculty in the nursing programs included in the sample required placement of students in actual work settings to provide the student the opportunity to meet course objectives. Seven percent of respondents identified the need for facilities with the capacity to place students in a clinical setting.

In this situation most professors were able to follow the planned course structure and utilize local resources such as hospitals and community agencies in a normal manner. A small number of faculty found some course modifications were required because of the lack of availability and/or access to standard types of facilities.

Since off-campus courses are taught at a site generally near the student's home or place of employment the placements for practical (clinical) experience are often at nearby locations. While this may provide for in-depth exposure to that particular setting and personnel, it does not provide the opportunity for diversity of experience in a new setting. Creativity in establishing appropriate experiences can be challenging and rewarding. It can also be a potential resource for future placements, even for the campus programs.

Access and convenience to appropriate library facilities is a fundamental requirement for effective delivery of academic courses. Faculty were queried regarding this with the following results: 26% no library containing appropriate materials; 48%: appropriate and convenient library; 26%: library available but difficult for the students to utilize.

It is notable that over one-half of the faculty surveyed did not have access to a library containing appropriate materials or that was convenient for student use. Because off-campus courses are often located at sites which do not have this built-in resource, it is understandable that this obstacle exists. Some remedies to this situation may be instructors loaning from their personal libraries, the home campus library assuming responsibility for adequate resources of this type, and reliance on other institutions in the area to provide these services. Another factor to be considered is student access. Since the off-campus courses may be taught on a once a week evening schedule, this may be the only time the student is at this site. The library hours may be a determining factor in the use of this resource. If the library closes at the same time class ends, the possibility of use may be eliminated.

One of the course supports that would appear to be difficult to provide for an off-campus course is computer access. In addition, the use of computers (or computer terminals) seems to be expanding in all types of courses. An item was included in the survey to determine whether computer facilities were available and appropriate. Most faculty, 74%, responded that computer facilities were not necessary for their course. For those who used computer facilities, 55% reported that they were satisfactory. That means, however, that 45% indicated they were dissatisfied with the computer facilities or had to modify their course because of the computer facilities. The results were approximately the same for both the Chapman and non-Chapman sample segments. With anticipated increased computer use in all fields, this is certainly a course resource that will impact on more programs and effective delivery.

It was an assumption of the authors that library services, computer facilities and clinical facilities were general examples or course supports. The previous data reflects the individual faculty perspectives for each of those categories. A non-specific question about course supports and the impact of these course supports on the student's ability to meet the course objectives was included. The results were 49% of the faculty believed the supports enhanced, 43% believed to supports did not affect and 8% believed supports inhibited the objectives. The non-Chapman College sub-set reported quite different perspectives with 37% reporting enhanced learning and 20% reporting that course supports inhibited learning.

These results are somewhat surprising when considering the previous findings regarding library and computer facilities where almost half of applicable responses expressed some dissatisfaction. Of the sample only a minority considered the supports to be detractors from meeting the course objectives. It leads to the question: What did the faculty consider to be course supports? The researchers did not ask this question. It would seem to be important to discover the answer in future research.

The sample was heavily represented by Chapman College faculty. Chapman programs employ Center Directors who provide a degree of full time continuity to off-campus programs, providing both faculty and students a feeling of having a home-base albeit one far from the home campus. The non-Chapman responses reflect more faculty operating in off-campus locations more likely without administrative personnel.

The degree of learning that occurs in any setting is difficult to measure. To compare the learning between two groups is even more intangible, but professors who have had experience teaching both in on-campus and off-campus settings, especially after a number of semesters, develop a sense about the achievements of students within the class. The measures maybe objective: tests and grades, or they may be subjective: discussion content or questions asked.

The sample was queried regarding the perspectives of student learning in an off-campus course compared to a similar on-campus course: 35% learned more; 56% learned the same; and 8% learned less. The percentage results were fairly consistent within each of the faculty sub-groups. From this data it appears that faculty perceive most off-campus students learn at least the same or more than students in similar on-campus courses. In pondering the meaning of this, the recurrent theme of motivated students anxious to use practical knowledge comes to mind.

Conclusions

Faculty teaching off-campus courses and participating in this survey overwhelmingly support the concept of off-campus courses or programs. They perceive that students learn the same or more as in similar on-campus courses, although learning may be a function of the mature and motivated student typically found in off-campus courses. Additional research should be undertaken to consider the level of student abilities and the level of motivation as compared to some measure of actual learning achievement beyond just faculty perception.

Faculty generally reported that off-campus courses were scheduled for convenience and not necessarily for the best educational techniques. Additional concern for good pedagogy should be blended with convenience in planning off-campus courses.

Support for the faculty in off-campus courses is a central aspect of this study. Two areas of support, computer facilities and library facilities, were selected as being potentially crucial elements in a quality program. Almost 50% of the faculty surveyed expressed concern over the level of support in regard to computer and/or library facilities but the level of learning by the students was still reported as equal to or greater than similar on campus courses. The two concepts were not linked on the questionnaire. A survey of faculty directly asking what support services are needed for a quality off-campus program might provide a stronger link between supports and quality.

Addendum

The research regarding off-campus faculty perspectives has continued since the original paper and the number of faculty responding has almost doubled to 322. The number of responses from Nursing faculty has not increased. Identifying faculty teaching off-campus continues to be very difficult.

The new data has diluted the strong Chapman factor regarding whether faculty responding chose to call themselves "practitioners" or "academicians". Fifty-six percent of the respondents identify themselves as academics and only 44% are practitioners. A few respondents prefer to be identified as both. Some evidence suggests that more faculty are teaching off-campus as part of their regular teaching assignment instead of as adjunct or for extra compensation.

The responses regarding the overall perspective on learning has changed. The faculty report that 31% learned more, 58% learned the same, and 11% learn less in an off-campus course as compared to an on-campus course.

The responses regarding the availability of a library indicates some changes. The percentage of faculty reporting no appropriate library available has decreased from 26% to 19%. The faculty reporting that an appropriate library was available and convenient decreased very little from 48% to 46%. The largest change was among faculty that reported an appropriate library was available, but it was difficult for students to use (an increase from 26% to 35%). Table 1 compares the responses about library availability and the faculty perceptions of learning. There is a specific influence where there is no appropriate library or a difficult to use library. The responses of learned-less are more than twice that where the library service was thought to be acceptable by the faculty.

Table 1

Library Availability Versus Learning Perceptions

	No Appropriate Library	Library Acceptable	Library Hard to Use
Learned More	27%	34%	28%
Learned Same	58%	60%	56%
Learned Less	15%	6%	16%
	N = 45	N = 137	N = 112

The computer availability question reveals some additional movement in the perceived need for computers in off-campus courses. The percentage of faculty reporting that a computer was not necessary for their course has declined from 74% to 70%. The resulting 30% of the faculty who want computers is probably too low a computer penetration into course formats based on a current survey of computer use (Frand and Britt, 1989). The satisfaction level of those using computers has also slipped to 50% reporting that they used computers in a normal manner in their course. Table 2 reveals a disproportionate number of learned-less responses from faculty who reported that computer availability was not adequate.

Table 2

Computer Availability Versus Learning

	Computer Not Needed	Normal Use	Course Modified	Computer Not Adequate
Learned More	31%	37%	8%	32%
Learned Same	58%	52%	84%	42%
Learned Less	11%	11%	8%	26%
	N = 205	N = 46	N = 26	N = 19

Current perspectives of the impact of course supports reveal 45% feel they enhanced, 46% say they had no affect, and 9% report they inhibited the quality of the course.

The conclusions that course supports, represented by library and computer access, have a specific affect on the perception of faculty continues to be supported by this survey. Faculty report lower levels of learning when the supports are perceived as a problem.

References

Cook, M.L.W. & Cook, J.E. (1984). Perceptions of regular versus adjunct faculty on five program factors. *Proceedings of the Seventh Annual Conference -- Quality in Off-campus Credit Programs: Today's Issues and Tomorrow's Prospects, 15*, 46-54.

Frand, J. L. & Britt, J. A. (1989). *Sixth Annual UCLA Survey of Business School Computer Usage.* Los Angeles, CA: University of California, Los Angeles.

Herzberg, F., Mausner, B., & Snyderman, B.B. (1959). *The motivation to work.* New York: Wiley.

Kansas State University. (1984). *Proceedings of the Seventh Annual Conference -- Quality in Off-Campus Credit Programs: Today's Issues and Tomorrow's Prospects, 15.*

Johnson, S.E. (1985). Faculty perspectives on outreach teaching. *Lifelong Learning, 9,* 11,13.

Scott, H.A. (1984). Compensating faculty members in nontraditional programs: A new approach. *Educational Record, 65,* 6-10.

Seldin, C.A. (1986). Faculty rewards for off-campus teaching: Weak at best. *Educational Horizons, 64,* 145-147.

Note

[1] The Cooks' paper was presented at the third Off-campus Library Services Conference, Reno, Nevada, and appeared in the 1987 edition of the conference proceedings.

Instructional Resources Support as a Function of Off-campus Library Services[1]

Richard H. Potter

Since 1974, Central Michigan University has conducted as extensive program for delivery of library materials to off-campus students. A major feature of that program is the reference librarians who visit courses and instruct students on the use of the program borrowing system, libraries in general, tools that are of particular use in the students' curriculum, and tools of particular use in the subject matter of the course. These same librarians are available by phone for consultation or individual student questions, including questions related to research topics for courses or for the independent project which represents the culmination of the extended master's degree program. The program is currently pursued by approximately seven thousand students in seventeen states and the Province of Ontario. An increasingly valuable service provided by these librarians is the provision of bibliographic searches, which are conducted at no cost for registered students.

Another notable feature of the program is the provision of a borrowing service that allows students to call the Central Michigan University library via a WATS line and order texts and serials. These requests are normally sent out within twenty-four hours, and students have several weeks to send back texts and may keep the photocopies of journal articles. The service is provided at no additional charge to admitted students, and the only direct cost to the student is the cost of mailing back monographs. In a recent month, over five thousand such requests were filled.

The librarians have also inventoried the library resources near each of the fifty centers where instruction is currently offered and provide information to students on materials and services that are available locally. If indexes are not readily available locally, Central Michigan University will provide them and will provide each center with one or more copies of the Central Michigan University catalog in microfiche form and with microfiche readers. In the spring of 1987, it is anticipated that students will be able to search the Central Michigan University catalog and order using their home or office computers and a modem.

Since its inception, the library program has provided services to faculty as well. The librarians, working with on-campus faculty, have developed extensive bibliographies for each of the graduate level courses which are provided to students at registration. At the request of faculty, the librarian will develop bibliographies on special topics. Faculty may also request reserve collections to be placed at a site where they are teaching, and the librarians will arrange for the collection.

Early in 1986, the library program undertook to provide an expanded set of services to faculty as a part of a general program to improve the quality of off-campus programs. Though not all aspects of that project are complete, this is a report of those plans and an indication of how a traditional campus library may serve as a significant factor in the quality of academic programs away from the campus in yet another way.

A substantial proportion of the faculty who teach in Central Michigan University's external programs are professionals who work for a government agency or private corporation. Although the vast majority possess terminal degrees in the area in which they are teaching, they do not currently hold an academic appointment at another institution. As a result, they are not in the "academic network" and thus often do not have access to new texts and materials that are coming out. There is no question about the qualifications of the individuals who are teaching, since their academic and vocational backgrounds are scrutinized most carefully by the academic departments on campus. However, since they may have been away from the academic world for some period of time, they may not be totally familiar with all of the texts, cases and other instructional materials that have been developed in recent years. In order to provide them access to such materials, the Central Michigan University Library Program has undertaken to acquire and circulate materials for review.

Textbooks

Central Michigan University has arranged to receive from selected publishers copies of texts which are appropriate for the course being taught in the extended degree program. The publishers were selected by a committee of faculty as those who are most likely to publish texts for courses offered in the external program. Publishers' representatives have been provided with course descriptions of courses being taught and asked to provide copies of texts which they believe to be appropriate. There is a significant incentive for the publishers' representatives to respond to this request, since the extended program is currently offering almost a thousand graduate courses per year. Consequently, the response from the publishers has been excellent. Periodically, a list of new additions is generated for each course and is sent to those faculty members who are approved to teach a particular course. Any promotional literature produced by the publisher describing the text is also sent with the list. A comprehensive list of all texts which have been received for each course is also available for faculty and is culled periodically to remove texts that are not being used or which have become dated. Faculty are then free to order texts to preview by calling the toll free number that was established to serve the student.

Case Studies

Case studies often play a major part of a graduate level management program, and Central Michigan University's extended program represents no exception to this rule. Once again, however, the adjunct faculty are not in the "network" and therefore often are unaware of new case studies that are being made available. Consequently, they may only use a limited number of case studies in their teaching.

A committee of faculty is in the process of reviewing a large number of cases which appear applicable to the courses offered through the extended degree program. Once identified, lists of these cases will be made available to each of the faculty members approved to teach the course, and copies will be obtained from the publishers in order that they may be circulated for preview. Case catalogs are also available for faculty review, as is information on how to use cases to their best advantage. The library staff also instructs faculty on the process of making cases available to the classes, and can offer suggestions on how cases may be used.

Computer Software

The library will notify software companies which produce products operating on MS-DOS of Central Michigan University's interest in assisting our faculty by allowing for the preview of instructional materials. The library program will request demonstration diskettes in all areas where the software might be applicable to extended degree courses. Descriptions and promotional literature of available software will then be sent to faculty who have been approved to teach courses for which the software appears appropriate. Faculty will then be able to preview the demonstration diskettes at their leisure by calling the toll free number that is used for ordering library materials. Should a faculty member decide to use a piece of software in his or her course, information as to how it may be ordered, discounts for multiple copies and other information will be available from the library program. The library program is also collecting published reviews of the software that are available for preview and will send these out with the diskettes as they are available.

Faculty Development

A final area in which the library will provide assistance to faculty in the Extended Degree Program is through the provision of faculty development materials. As was mentioned above, since a number of faculty in the Extended Degree Program are adjunct faculty who are drawn from the ranks of highly qualified professionals, they may not have ready access to or be acquainted with publications that will be of assistance to them in improving their style of teaching or methods of delivery of materials. Given the intensive scheduling patterns used in the extended degree program, creative use of instructor contact time is necessary in order to insure that students receive full benefit of the available classroom time. Thus, this aspect of the faculty support system is viewed as a major contributor to increasing the quality of the Extended Degree Program.

In order to accomplish this objective, the library program has undertaken to collect faculty development materials. The first priority has been materials which stress "how-to" aspects of classroom teaching and are primarily directed at those faculty who are practitioners, although the collection is available to all faculty and to the on-campus faculty. The process by which this task will be completed consists of four steps:

1. Identification of and examination of materials already possessed by the Central Michigan University library
2. Identification and collection of materials from new sources (e.g., the Center for Faculty Development at Kansas State University)
3. Promotion of the collection

4. Circulation of the material

The identification of the materials which already exist in the Central Michigan University library has already begun as has the identification of new sources of material. It is expected that this phase of the program will be well underway when a new regional librarian is employed in January, 1987, whose additional "bibliographic" assignment will be the development of a collection of materials. As with the circulation of library materials to off-campus students, the key to the success of the program is seen as the promotion of the service to faculty. This will be accomplished through direct mailing, the newsletter that is sent to adjunct faculty, "The Faculty Update," and through the contract which is sent to each accomplished through the same mechanism as the circulation of the library's main collection to the extended student body--the WATS line ordering system.

Summary

The Extended Degree Program views the library component as a vital ingredient in the total program and one which materially affects the quality of the degree program. As such, it is appropriate that the library program take part in a general effort to increase the overall quality of the academic offerings. Since quality of instruction is one of the variables which most directly impacts the quality of the program, the instructional support system will be a mechanism through which the library can have the largest impact on the program. With a mechanism already in place to circulate materials at a distance and to provide the service, the library is in the most logical position to take on this role. Further, the addition of this new service has further enhanced the position of the library program in the Extended Degree Program.

Note

[1] Dr. Potter's paper was presented at the third Off-campus Library Services Conference, Reno, Nevada, and appeared in the 1987 edition of the conference proceedings.

Additional information about the program of instructional support articulated by Dr. Potter was provided in the 1989 conference proceedings with the article prepared by Maryhelen Garrett.

Garrett, M. (1989). Going to the Head of the Class: The Development and Implementation of an Instructional Materials Support Collection for Off-campus Faculty. In B.M. Lessin (Ed.), *The Off-campus Library Services Conference Proceedings* (pp.134-155). Mount Pleasant, MI: Central Michigan University.

Getting It Right Down Under:
Off-campus Library Services in Australia[1]

Christine Crocker

In preparing this paper, I spent some hours reading the North American literature on off-campus library services. I know the Australian scene well and I am reasonably familiar with practices in Britain; I have corresponded with some librarians in the U.S. and Canada but I had not visited any libraries in those countries. I looked particularly at the proceedings from the earlier conferences in 1982 and 1985 and I soon found that the papers presented at those sessions dealt with concerns and problems familiar to Australian librarians. I was facing the same dilemma as John Weatherford, when at the 1982 conference, he announced: "In such an assembly as this, where innovators are the rule, I must pick my way gingerly lest I tell you merely what you already know." (p. 35)

I felt you didn't require a theoretical paper from a visiting Aussie--you have already met to discuss issues such as effects of academic programs on library services; technology advances; evaluation of services; bibliographic instruction. So my paper will give an outline of my own experience in the off-campus area; some background into the development of off-campus library services in Australia; and a summary of what we have achieved in the last ten years and what we still have ahead of us.

Introduction

I first became involved with distance education in 1964, when my family moved from Victoria to Queensland and I moved from a large secondary school to a small one; from a choice of courses to no choice. In order to continue Latin, I enrolled as a student with the Queensland Secondary correspondence School. Every fortnight I received bulky books of notes with exercises for completion and submission as homework. This experience, combined as it was with a failure at the end of the two year period, convinced me that off-campus study is *not* easy!

My next experience was with the Library Association of Australia's Registration Examination which I began in 1966. I successfully passed three examinations at the end of that year; no doubt a small wonder, as the only help available in each course consisted of a syllabus, a reading list and past examination papers. I didn't attempt to complete Registration until 1975 and 1976 when I sat for the remaining six examinations. I'm sure my maturity at that time, plus an increased awareness that any study required discipline, effort and hours helped me to achieve the credits and distinctions on those final papers. So by the time I had my close encounter of the third kind, I was well prepared. This was as foundation External Studies Librarian at the College of Advanced Education in Townsville, North Queensland.

Three Australian Services

Townsville is 1,000 miles from Brisbane, the state capital of Queensland, and it is the second largest city in Queensland. The college mainly offered teacher training courses, supplementing these with Diplomas in business studies and community welfare. In 1977, the first "off-campus" courses began, but still within a classroom situation. Lecturers traveled on a weekly basis to study centres in Mackay and Cairns, each 250 miles south and north, respectively, of Townsville.

Four hours of class contact occurred each week, and library delivery was simple: the students would request books which were packed into sturdy suitcases and carried to each class by the lecturer. By 1978, the college was ready to offer fully external courses and enrolled an initial intake of sixty-eight students, all teachers wishing to upgrade their existing qualifications. In Barton Lessin's foreword to the 1982 conference he commented that Central Michigan University librarians associated with off-campus programs sometimes felt they "were working in a void" (p. 2). It was much the same at Townsville CAE; although off-campus programs had been a part of Australian higher education for seventy years, there were few people who could advise us from the perspective of starting courses, and setting up associated policies and procedures.

We met the challenges of the occasion with enthusiasm, and some of our experiments at this time included the establishment of five study centres in North Queensland, complete with small collections of books, journals and audiovisual equipment; the provision of books through reproduction on microfiche; conducting off-campus reader education classes; involvement of the librarian in the preparation of courses; and the supply of "browsing pages" --photocopied contents and index pages of selected titles, annual indexes from crucial journals, and relevant extracts from periodical indexes. It's true that some of those experiments fell by the wayside--for example that of supplying recommended texts on microfiche where we encountered delays and difficulties with copyright, and also a reasonable degree of user resistance!

However, others were particularly successful such as those "browsing" pages which were labor intensive to produce but very popular with students who wanted to made an informed choice before requesting material from the off-campus service. The Library Guide, produced in a looseleaf format with regular updates was also popular, and was commended as being of a high standard by the Australian Library Promotions Council, in its annual Public Relations Awards.

The College clearly defined the role of the External Studies Librarian, stressing the following functions:

1.   to act as an identifiable person to whom students can confidently write or phone concerning bibliographical and resource materials problems;
2.   to liaise with external studies lecturers on all matters of resource provision for external students;
3.   to meet with students to discuss problems, provide reader education programs etc.;
4.   to prepare guides for external students;
5.   to develop and review policies of resource provision.

The small number of students enrolled in those first years made it very easy for me to establish and maintain personal contact with them, and it was even possible to visit most of them. as in those days intake was restricted to Queensland and drawn mainly from areas in north Queensland. Years later I met someone in Brisbane who remembered me--she had been one of those students, she regarded the college and the library with affection, and attributed her success in the off-campus program mainly to the friendly contact maintained by the library and her lecturers.

As Thatcher Librarian

The situation at the University of Queensland was a little different: after all, there are 2,000, students not sixty-eight! The University was a pioneer in the development of distance teaching in Australia and remained the sole provider of external studies within that state until the colleges entered the field during the 1970's. In 1949 the University transformed its separate external studies unit into a fully fledged academic department. At that time the Thatcher Memorial Library was created, so named as a tribute to a past Director of External Studies at the University. The collection remained a part of the Department of External Studies until 1960 when the staff and the collection came under the aegis of the University Library. By the time I joined the University of Queensland staff in 1980, Thatcher Library was housed on the ground floor of a four-storied building, with the other three floors occupied by the Undergraduate Library. Now the University has entered a new phase in its external programs by adopting an integrated approach; the School of External Studies and Continuing Education has separate premises, but academic staff have joined their colleagues in other Schools; courses are prepared during a secondment to the School and offered by an increasing number of faculties.

Let me tell you a little bit about the operation of Thatcher Library. It is one of the seventeen branches that form the University of Queensland library. It has a staff of ten, and a collection of around 100,000 items, mainly books but also cassette tapes, some kits, and a collection of photocopied journal articles. The library opens to users six days a week from 12:45 to 4:45 p.m.; on weekdays the morning hours are devoted to sending out materials in response to telephone and postal requests.

Its main function is to operate a postal service to the remote off-campus students, though this service is not restricted by geographic location and is available to any student enrolled in the off-campus mode. Material is sent to students through a courier service operated by Australia Post; students must return the material at their own cost. Around 28,000 postal loans are sent from the library. Photocopies are provided for student retention on a voucher system: $1.50 guarantees supply of any journal article, and postage to the student's home. The library operates an answering phone service for after-hour queries, and it shares a toll-free line with the School of External Studies. Thatcher opens for extended hours during any of the voluntary residential schools held on the campus, and its collection is no longer exclusively for use by external students as on-campus students are permitted overnight loan privileges.

Similarly, the off-campus service is no longer limited to the collection held in Thatcher; library staff also provide books and photocopies from the University's total library resources. Reader education is provided by specialist staff in the Central and Undergraduate libraries; interlibrary loans and on-line literature searches are available, again from the Central Library. This referral does little to promote professional goodwill. Ironically the Thatcher staff now seem to have "second-class" status; they are able to meet standard requests; liaise with academics; develop and know the collection; but the more challenging reference questions are handed over to other staff, often quite remote from the processes of external tracking, and the off-campus students.

The staff work in three teams of librarian and library assistant and each team assumes responsibility for fulfilling requests, ordering materials, advising students and liaising with teaching staff, within certain subject areas. Theoretically this guarantees expert knowledge of collection and ensures the library staff are aware of course and assignment requirements, and that they liaise regularly and effectively with academics. Each team receives all course material and related information sent to students; the three librarians are also members of the Council of External Studies. The Thatcher Librarian is a member of the Council and of the board of External Studies and Continuing Education; while I was there, I was also elected to the Board's Executive.

While the librarians in Thatcher do build up expert knowledge about the library's resources, successful liaison with academic staff is largely related to the personality, expertise and enthusiasm of the librarian concerned. During my four years as the Thatcher Librarian, I felt that the Thatcher staff could have adopted a more dynamic role in course preparation. However, I acknowledge that this type of involvement is often dependent on the academic concerned, and at the University of Queensland, with so much change occurring in the 1980's, we battled cautiously and gradually to win over staff with somewhat entrenched ideas and could only foreshadow the concept of the value of a librarian during the course-writing process.

Thatcher Library is now unique in Australia; no other library maintains a separate collection for external students. In his annual report for 1985, the Librarian at the University of Queensland said:

Coverage of wanted material by Thatcher stock seems to be

declining.... For many years there has been a great deal of
formal and informal evidence that Thatcher Library is highly
regarded by external students. Its success has been
substantially due to its existence as a separate collection
tailored to the needs of external courses .... In 1985
Thatcher staff spent 194 hours visiting other libraries to seek
references, borrow books and make photocopies. (p. 22-23)

Given figures such as these, it is understandable that the University has
considered integration of the Thatcher service. Yet in a library system
of seventeen branches, there seems little advantage in merging one,
and the one with a readily identifiable clientele of two thousand.

Without a doubt, working in Thatcher enabled the staff to establish a
very strong and good relationship with the University's off-campus
students. The end of the year always brought a flood of visits, calls,
gifts, letters and cards, all conveying gratitude. That role of general
guidance and counseling (Lessin, 1982, p. 47), is one that is time-
consuming, impossible to record statistically, but overwhelmingly
appreciated by the students, as demonstrated by comments taken from
student letters: "The feeling of belonging engendered by the Thatcher
staff in those who have no other personal contact with the University
makes the entire burden of external studying not only bearable, but
pleasant." "Your unfailing courtesy and promptness amazes me--
especially towards students like me who usually want too much, too
late." "To come to know so many people who are dedicated, helpful,
kind and knowledgeable has been the highlight of my experience with
the University."

At Deakin

Against this background, it was with some trepidation that I renewed
my acquaintance with off-campus library services when I joined Deakin
as its Reader Services Librarian in 1985. Deakin is Australia's newest
University, and it specializes in off-campus courses for undergraduate
and higher degrees. It is becoming particularly famous for its off-
campus MBA and PhD programs.

The Library has a staff of around sixty, pretty equally divided between
Technical Services and Reader Services. I have six professional
librarians and a library technician in the Reference section, and one
librarian and one library technician full time in the Off-campus

section--and this in an institution with 4,800 off-campus and 2,300 on-campus students.

Within Victoria, there is a co-operative group called CAVAL (Co-operative Action for Victorian Academic Libraries) and one of CAVAL's activities is to support a reciprocal borrowing program whereby students at one institution can borrow from the libraries of other institutions. The three city-based Universities are still a little conservative, and don't allow undergraduate students of other institutions to borrow; luckily one is a little more lenient towards off-campus undergraduate students, and extends borrowing privileges. Elsewhere in Australia, some libraries allow borrowing privileges to off-campus students enrolled at other institutions, and I'll mention this again a little later.

Table 1

Deakin Off-campus Students, as of April 30th, 1986

Melbourne area	1613	33.4%
Interstate	1451	30.0%
Victoria	892	18.4%
Geelong region	789	16.3%
Overseas	91	1.9%
Total	4836	100.0%

Certainly, a high proportion of Deakin's off-campus students have personal access to a tertiary library. Of the total external enrollment, this year about thirty percent have used the off-campus service offered by the Library. In 1985, 19,000 loans were requested through the off-campus service.

It's a good service. Deakin responds to telephone, postal, personal, telex, facsimile and electronic mail requests for materials, and sends that material to off-campus students around the world. Those living within Australia receive the material by overnight courier delivery, and are able to return it in the same fashion at no cost: Deakin pays delivery costs both ways. Airmail is used by students resident overseas,

overseas, and the library reimburses students for return airmail costs. Photocopies of journal articles are sent out free of charge; and students may borrow videotapes and audio cassettes as well as books.

Deakin has an on-line catalogue system which provides circulation information. When the student makes a telephone inquiry, the librarian can access the catalogue; confirm that the requested titles are available or on loan; and place reservations as necessary. Subject searches can be carried out on the spot, with the student able to make a choice of material, which is then forwarded by the courier service. The Library ran an experiment in 1984, involving a toll-free line and access at advertised times to a librarian at the end of that line using the on-line catalogue. I preferred to merge the service into the routine work of all reference librarians; this seems a natural feature in an institution with over half its students off-campus. The Library opens throughout the academic year until 10:00 p.m. each evening (but only until 6:00 p.m. on Fridays) and from 1:00 p.m. to 5:00 p.m. each Saturday and Sunday. The telephone from the off-campus area is switched through to the reference desk, so that students have access to specialist staff outside normal business hours.

On-line literature searches are also available free of charge to all students, and this service is particularly popular with research students, who can then request the abstracted material from Deakin or through our interlibrary loan service.

The off-campus service at Deakin is increasing its demands on staff time, and on the collection. It has been necessary this year to supplement professional staffing, and for four days each week one of the reference librarians spends the day in the off-campus area, answering telephone inquiries and handling the subject related requests. No doubt you know these non-specific requests, and the time they can absorb; requests such as:

- everything on the Bible
- send me something on the short story
- please send me a biography
- can I have enough information on this topic to make sure I pass the exam
- I want some stuff on technology
- fraud in science please
- anything on broadcasting, journalism, radio technology and the media.

This daily secondment of reference staff has helped the integration of the service. Reference staff are gaining a better understanding of the off-campus service and of the students. Next year I propose to lengthen the secondments, so that one person spends up to three months, primarily dealing with off-campus requests.

Regional Study Centres

The University of Queensland operates the most sophisticated network of study centres in Australia. They are all in Queensland, and in eight of these there is a collection of library resources. These collections are known as the Ringrose libraries, again as a memorial tribute to a former Director of External Studies. The collections now have a total of 22,000 items and 45 periodical titles, centrally processed by the University Library. In each Centre, a librarian is employed for up to ten hours each week, and students are encouraged to use the Centre for loans, study, tutorials and as an information centre.

Some of the centres are shared by other institutions; their commitment ranges from occasional visits and the supply of information brochures, to sharing the costs of maintenance of the centre, and contributing to the resources of the library and the salary of the local librarian. This is a great improvement over conditions existing before 1982; with no formal agreement between all the institutions, each jealously guarded its "own" belongings. In one centre, shared by four institutions, there were four separate collections; one was classified by Library of Congress, two by Dewey and the other arranged by title. Two of the institutions provided card catalogues of the material held in the centre; the third provided a computer-printed listing; the fourth did not catalogue their material! Each institution paid the part-time local librarian for a varying number of hours, on varying salary scales. It was a great day when, finally, agreement was achieved; books were interfiled; catalogues were combined; the librarians were paid by the University of Queensland and the other institutions contributed a proportion of recurrent costs of the centres to the University.

By 1984, when the study centres and Ringrose libraries had been brought under closer control by the University, I had produced a standard Ringrose procedures manual as a looseleaf appendix to the Study Centre Guide produced by the School. I had visited every centre, most of them annually; it was obvious that the role of the study centre librarian had changed with co-operative use of the centres. The local librarians are often the only people on duty in the Centre at the advertised opening times.   They are confronted with questions on specific subjects, courses, career planning, quotas, tertiary enrollment procedures, etc. In this I felt they needed some guidance and training, and I will return to this point.

Deakin also operates study centres within Victoria; these are mostly at regional colleges and the library has deposited small core collections within the college or local public library. Those books in effect become the property of that library, and are integrated into the library's own collection and catalogue.

There is now discussion on the development of national network of study centres, based on existing colleges of Technical and Further Education; already TAFE colleges are often operating as a support centre in small towns, and this seems a natural extension in use of their facilities and local presence.

Australia--As It Was

A push for external enrollments occurred in the 1970's and by the end of that decade external programs were a notable feature of Australian colleges, for the quite simple reason that funding for higher education was perceived to be based on the number of enrollments (Johnson, p. 5).   In the 1979-81 triennium, external enrollments at tertiary institutions increased by 30% and by 1982, external students formed 12% of *all* enrollments.

But external tertiary courses made a much earlier entry than this. The University of Queensland was the first Australian institution to become involved with distance education, with provision for this in its Establishment Act of 1909. It enrolled its first external students in 1911, with three of the total enrollment of 83 being off-campus. It now has an annual enrollment of about 18,000 and of those 2,050 or around 11% are off-campus.

Table 2

Students by Type of Enrollment at Selected Institutions in 1985

	Total external enrollment	Total enrollment	% External
Universities, External			
New England	5997	8800	68.2%
Deakin	4427	6698	66.1%
Murdoch	1413	3987	35.4%
Macquarie	1645	11573	14.2%
Queensland	2046	17948	11.4%
Advanced Institutes within Universities			
Wollongong	607	1774	34.2%
James Cook	368	1186	31.0%
Colleges			
Armidale CAE	1385	1933	71.7%
Gippsland IAE	2004	2939	68.2%
Mitchell CAE	3274	4883	67.0%
Riverina-Murray IHE	3902	6040	64.6%
Warrnambool IAE	1169	1936	60.4%
Darling Downs IAE	2933	5261	55.7%
Capricornia IAE	1636	3035	53.9%
South Australia IAE	2702	11120	24.3%
Tasmania State I.T.	597	2612	22.9%
Brisbane CAE	1104	8157	13.5%
Western Australia CAE	1266	9775	13.0%
Western Australia I.T.	1218	12485	9.8%
Darwin I.T.	89	1160	7.7%
R.M.I.T.	803	10958	7.3%

Source: *CTEC Selected University Statistics* and *Selected Advanced Education Statistics for 1985*).

Four other universities, from Australia's total of nineteen, offer
external courses with the University of New England (Armidale,
N.S.W.) enrolling students since its autonomy in 1955; Macquarie
(Sydney, N.S.W.) since its inception in 1967; Murdoch (Perth, W.A.)
in 1975, and Deakin (Geelong, Victoria) being the latest arrival, since
its foundation in 1978. During World War II, the Universities of
Sydney and Melbourne offered external courses too, but were quick to
surrender those in the early postwar period. However, today five other
universities still have some external or distance students enrolled; they
don't offer external courses, but do enroll distance students and do so
without adequate support services.

College development began with courses offered from the Royal
Melbourne Institute of Technology in 1919; these too were designed
to cater to cater to the need of returned servicemen. In 1962 Adelaide
Teachers' College began off-campus study, followed in 1968 by the
Western Australian Institute of Technology. And then in the 1970's
Australia experienced the same great surge into external studies as
occurred in the States (Houle, 1974, p. 1) with many colleges,
particularly those in regional centres, offering programs in the off-
campus mode.

Our Achievements to Date

Given that historical background, Australia had a belated burst of
activity into this sphere of librarianship. There had been very little
professional literature published on library services to external students
when I co-authored one in 1978; we found some descriptive articles,
mainly about Thatcher Library. From then on the situation improved,
and rapidly. 1979 saw the first survey on services to external students
(Store, 1981), which at last gathered much needed information; the
dissemination of the results helped clarify the variations in service then
occurring around Australia. At the biennial conference of the Library
Association of Australia (LAA) in that same year, a small group of
enthusiasts used the results of that survey as the basis for discussion at
a workshop on "The Library in Distance Education." That same group
became the foundation of the Association's Special Interest Group on
Distance Education, ratified in November 1979. The Group has
around 600 members.

Guidelines are Prepared

In 1981 as Convenor of the Group, I organized the first national workshop on library services in distance education. The emphasis on this two-day workshop lay with the group sessions, where participants bore the responsibility for drafting guidelines for adequacy in the provision of library resources and services in distance education programs. Groups focused on different topics, and presented written drafts on:

1. staffing
2. materials provision
3. finances
4. services
5. co-operative study centres
6. accommodation
7. audiovisual materials
8. public library liaison.

From there, I applied to the LAA for special funding, to ensure development of those preliminary drafts through to final guidelines. This funding was granted in 1982, and a small working group of seven was established. We met four times between February and August that year, and we used the statements from the workshop groups as the basis for our deliberations. In 1982 we published the *Guidelines for Library Services to External Students* as qualitative statements recommending the minimum level of provision for library services to students enrolled in the external mode with any post-secondary institution within Australia.

So how influential has that document been? In 1985 I conducted a survey of thirty-six academic institutions offering external courses, seeking information on the recognition and use of the professionally-approved *Guidelines*. Thirty institutions responded; of those twenty-seven were aware of the publication, but only eight had used the *Guidelines* to evaluate their services and resources for off-campus students. Another eight intended to carry out that evaluation--as soon as time permitted. Until a library evaluates its service, by making its first priority the availability of staff time for a review, there can be no supported claims for increased financial resources, different library policies or changes in services or staffing levels. Of the eight

institutions who had evaluated their services, four had implemented
changes; one had not made any decision; another was restrained from
implementing new policies through lack of staff and funds; and two felt
change was not required--but significantly, one of those institutions had
use sections of the *Guidelines*, as successful support for
recommendations to the College administration on library staffing
levels.

Last year, at the seminar on library services in distance education held
in conjunction with the ICDE 13th World Conference, participants
unanimously recommended to the LAA that a copy of the *Guidelines*
be sent to the chief executive officers of each institution offering post-
secondary off-campus courses. At that stage, the publication was out
of print; however, a reprint occurred, and this action will now be taken.
A letter with each copy will seek feedback and recommendations, and
the Special Interest Group on Distance Education will use such
comments in consideration of a second copy will seek feedback and
recommendations, and the Special Interest Group on Distance
Education will use such comments in consideration of a second edition
of the *Guidelines*.

Table 3

Services Evaluated Against "Guidelines" (8 Responses)

Change implemented	Integration of much of the collection. Centralisation of some services. Changes to funding allocation arrangements. Staffing re-organization. Imposition of geographical limit on service. Major changes were implemented; but difficult to ascertain influence of *Guidelines* over other documents.
Change implemented	Greater use of telephone for contacting implemented external students. Pilot project using courier service to deliver materials. Changes implemented from reading *Guidelines* and the Deakin University survey.
Change implemented	Helped in decision to install '008' phone service. In many respects, service achieves points raised.
Change implemented	Changes made to lending and copyright policies, and to housing practices. Question of improved central responsibility for external studies at the college also examined, but without producing outcome. Collection integrated on open shelves, having been in closed access. Photocopies made in advance of courses were reduced and a policy of providing copies for retention introduced.
No change	No actual decision made by Library administration.
Change desired but not possible	Mainly through lack of staff and funds. Would have liked to implement more multiple copies of requested material and supply photocopies for retention.
Change not desired	Feel that existing policies adequately cater to students' needs.
Change not desired	Services already of adequate standard. Sections of *Guidelines* used to support recommendations on library staffing levels to college administration. Recommendations accepted by college.

"Open Sesame" for the Off-campus Student?

In 1982, the Commonwealth Tertiary Education Commission (CTEC) funded an investigation into student needs for reference material, the sources they use and the effects of the external system in which they study. This research was master-minded by Margaret Cameron, the Chief Librarian at Deakin and in 1983 *External Students and Their Libraries* (or the Winter/Cameron report as it is more commonly known) appeared. This publication provided librarians with the opportunity to compare student attitudes towards the library service provided by their home institution, with information on services available or possible, as described in Store's survey and the *Guidelines*. Librarians at last were able to evaluate the worth of some of the services offered, and of those not offered, and reapply their energies in an innovative way.

A feature of the survey was that sixty percent of the respondents chose to make further comments on the open ended final page. Of that sixty percent, almost one third mentioned particularly the need to have access to and borrowing rights from the libraries of geographically more convenient tertiary institutions than the one at which they were enrolled. Many suggested a special external student borrowing card, which would automatically entitle the holder to borrow from any tertiary library in Australia. As the report points out:

> One of the difficulties in implementing such an arrangement is the reluctance to participate which has been shown by many of the major university libraries in the capital cities. The involvement of these institutions would be crucial to the success of the venture, as a large proportion of students live in or near the capital cities and major towns, where colleges and universities are mostly located. More than half of the external students in Australia would be able to visit a nearer college or university. It is significant that three of the largest providers of external programs are located in large country towns, but with large concentrations of their external students in the state capital, from which the institution is rather remote. Yet external students in those capital cities are not eligible to borrow from the libraries of most of their local universities. One of the major concerns of these university libraries is a "flood" of external students. This study has shown that such a flood is unlikely. (p. 81-81)

Deakin is currently carrying out more research, again with special funding from CTEC. Earlier this year we surveyed the Chief Librarians of every Australian University, College of Advanced Education and College of Technical and Further Education. Issues addressed in our study include current policy and practice in lending to students of other institutions, the circumstances in which the libraries would permit visiting off-campus students to borrow, (identification, authorization, sanctions, financial compensation), and the mechanisms of co-operation.

We are still working on the final report, but anticipate that we will seek additional funds from CTEC to implement the recommendations of the report. We are confident that we can work out a system acceptable to the majority, if not all, of the tertiary institutions around Australia whereby off-campus students from other institutions will be registered as borrowers on presentation of positive identification and evidence of current enrollment at their home institution.

This access to tertiary libraries around Australia will be a high-step forward in providing off-campus students with the educational opportunities available to their on-campus colleagues.

Reader Education

I have been involved to some extent with reader education, or bibliographic instruction, for off-campus students in each of the three positions. At Townsville, I regularly traveled to the centres in Mackay and Cairns and held classes there; I prepared pathfinders and special guides and met with groups of students in other centres. Formal classes were possible during the compulsory residential schools. At Thatcher, I prepared guides and handouts, and organized classes during the voluntary schools on campus, and at Deakin, one of my staff is primarily responsible for reader education to both on-campus and off-campus students. She meets students or class contact during their residential weekends either at Deakin or in our study centre in Melbourne, and I sometimes join these gatherings.

In an effort to introduce our students to libraries and library resources, without featuring any particular library, this year we produced a video. In planning this, we recognized that external students use many other libraries in addition to those at the institutions at which they are enrolled. But access to a range of libraries is not enough; students also need to be able to use those libraries effectively. Reader education is needed which will equip students anywhere, enrolled in any institution, to use any library. As formal classes are not feasible for scattered off-campus students, a different strategy is necessary. With increased knowledge--and increased confidence--they can then approach their local library.

Our first video is intended as a pilot project, to test the feasibility of teaching search strategy and providing information on research resources within a specific subject area, in such a way that the knowledge can be generalized in many other libraries. This first one is devoted to Australian studies, and as well as including copies in our collection for our own students, we are selling copies to other libraries.

Coordination and Cooperation

CTEC has a Standing Committee on External Studies chaired by Richard Johnson, a Special Commissioner of CTEC, and author of the 1983 report, *The Provision of External Studies in Australian Higher Education.* That report highlighted the lack of national coordination and interstate cooperation in distance education, and suggested a range of possible mechanisms to resolve this. The Committee has mapped out several years' work, concentrating its attention on issues such as the production and distribution of course materials, cross-crediting, increased cost-effectiveness, and a nationwide network of learning centres.

One the library scene, we to need to focus on cooperation and coordination. Already the five universities involved in off-campus teaching are cooperating in an intra-institutional degree, where students may pick relevant subjects from any of the five, leading to successful completion of their degree from one. This has already produced some mild headaches for students and librarians, from little things like course guides arriving late and confused enrollment details, to the larger issue of library resources. The deal is that each institution will provide library support for the specific courses it offers, and meet the requests of all students enrolled in those courses, regardless of their "home-base" institution. This should work; it seems relatively simple. However, it does not take into account the widely varying library services between those five institutions. A major snare for Deakin students enrolled in one course at any of the other institutions, is that they often no longer receive library materials by overnight courier, and they always have to pay the return delivery costs.

Viatel: Australian videotex system

Viatel is Telecom Australia's public videotex service. Most of the information on Viatel is supplied by services providers who are responsible for deciding what they put on Viatel and how they present it. Deakin University is a provider, and has some basic screens about the University and the Library. There is also information on courses offered by Deakin.

Students can send messages to their lecturers, or confirm their enrollment, or request library materials through Viatel. If they don't already have Viatel access at home or at work, they now face increased opportunities of using a Viatel terminal at their local public library.

Prospective students can scroll through the course information, request brochures, make course-related inquiries and provisionally enroll.

What lies before us?

Many of our achievements to date have opened up further challenges to us. Will we be able to meet these?

The *Guidelines* now exist but it remains for librarians themselves to implement those recommendations on the minimum level of library support for off-campus students. It is the librarians who have now to evaluate, review, agitate, lobby, liaise, work, encourage, insist and utilize. Nobody will do it for us--and it must be fitted around already busy schedules.

I am hopeful and we have almost cracked the hard shell surrounding the soft issue of external students borrowing from other tertiary libraries. We now need to take these visiting rights a step further, and plan and coordinate an Australia-wide system of orientation sessions, and formal bibliographic instruction classes at these libraries, so that all students can learn how to exploit the wealth of information they contain. Deakin's video is a start in promoting this type of cooperation, but we still have a long road to travel.

As a group, Australian librarians have to ensure our voice is heard in discussions on the development of a national network of study centres, and of a database of educational opportunities. Colleges of Technical and Further Education (TAFE) may provide the basis for a national study centre network, but we need a coordinated survey of their practices and standards, leading to the preparation of some guidelines for the role of TAFE Colleges and their libraries as study centres for external students. It is of course quite unrealistic to suggest that these libraries can possibly provide collection support for the range of students in their locality. That role belongs quite firmly with the home institution, who may choose (or may even be encouraged) to deposit books relevant to their students' needs in some of the TAFE centres. Most TAFE libraries, however, need increased funding for support staff, to enable them to open libraries for longer and more suitable hours. They also need funding for improved communications, so that TAFE librarians can telephone or telex the students' home institution; participate in cooperative cataloguing and locations schemes for ease of direction of students; and maintain regular contact with the institutions enrolling the majority of students serviced by the TAFE centres.

There is a great need for a coordinated database of all courses available in the off-campus mode; indeed this need really is for all courses available to any/all students, but the need for accurate, up-to-date information on off-campus courses is the greater, due to the isolation of potential and current students, the distances separating them from institutions and educational counselling opportunities, and the bureaucratic and often bewildering enrollment procedures of most of our institutions! The development of a database needs funding, but most of all it needs coordination at a national level. I was most impressed with the ECCTIS system in operation from the Open University in England and I live in hope that Australia will be able to mount and support a similar system. Viatel has provided a significant start in meeting this need; CTEC has recognized the need for a database of external courses. I can see as an automatic development from this, that libraries and librarians will provide users with up-to-date, accurate information on educational opportunities. The development of libraries, particularly public libraries, as educational guidance centres is already an issue needing full exploration by appropriate groups; this need will grow as a database of courses becomes reality.

I believe the LAA needs to form a working group or a standing committee to monitor developments in adult education, distance education and educational guidance. Librarians in regional centres and small towns, and, particularly, librarians in cooperative study centres, will need training courses so they are able to respond to questions, provide information, seek answers. It should be possible for the LAA to seek professional expertise in the design of a training manual to equip librarians everywhere with a better ability to respond to adults seeking information on the range of educational opportunities now available to them. This is one of the challenges currently being addressed by that same group of enthusiasts in the Special Interest Group in Distance Education.

Conclusion

Off-campus studies may have begun in Australia in 1909, but they only came of age during the 1970's and maturity is now in sight with the related library services. After such a slow start, development has been rapid and astonishing. Australian institutions and their librarians have hurdled many obstacles, and built many sound structures. Challenges still lie ahead of us. I believe we will meet them with the same enthusiasm, energy and commitment that has been demonstrated so well in this part of the world.

Addendum: The Australian Scene for the 1990's

In 1988, the Federal Government released its policy statement on higher education, announcing the government's strategy for the long-term development of Australia's higher education system, including its commitment to the objective of fewer, larger institutions, brought about by amalgamation and consolidation. This paper also announced decisions on the rationalisation of distance education.

The policy includes proposals for enhancing the provision of external studies by reducing duplication, fostering cooperation between institutions and improving the overall quality, availability and efficiency of external studies courses (p. 49). In order to rationalise the production of external studies materials, the Government announced that there would be six Distance Education Centres (DECs), which would receive government funding to develop, produce and deliver off-campus courses. The selection of DECs would be undertaken on a competitive basis; institutions had to submit an expression of interest in designation as a DEC, and offers for DEC status would be made for a minimum period of five years, with renewal of DEC status subject to review. At the same time, the document stated that while the rates at which federal government funding would be made for external students were still to be determined after assessment of the costings included in institutional submissions, it was expected that the average total cost per student for external courses would be less than the rate for on-campus students. Furthermore the government proposed to establish a coordinating mechanism to assist in monitoring and reviewing external studies, comprising those institutions designated as DECs, other teaching institutions, and the government. This group, now known as NDEC, the National Distance Education Conference, will be charged with further rationalisation of courses among the DECs, as well as arrangements for filling gaps in the provision of courses, and for ensuring the development and delivery of programs of the highest quality, using advanced technologies.

A Period of Change

Australian academic institutions face massive re-organisation in the 1990's, with almost all involved in some merger. By the end of 1989, eight institutions had been named as distance education centres. The policy statement allows those institutions which are not designated DECs to retain some involvement in distance education as delivery-only institutions, using one of the nationally accepted course packages developed by a DEC. The development of distance education centres, a significant rationalisation of distance education providers, will allow an opportunity for achieving economies through large scale joint course development between institutions.

National coordination could foster the preparation of a common library guide for off-campus students; help in the organisation of a cost-effective, common courier delivery system; and in the development of collections and services to support off-campus students throughout Australia. This coordination looks far more possible in the 1990's; with the establishment of NDEC, the National Distance Education Conference. This body has already set up a number of working groups, investigating areas of off-campus provision, such as quality in external teaching, technological innovations, and database development. In this last area, the working group is devising proposals for a national database of course information; while of enormous benefit to present and potential students, this database will also help libraries plan collaborative ventures in collection development and user education.

Student Use of Other Libraries

Open borrowing from academic libraries received attention in 1986 when the Commonwealth Tertiary Education Commission funded a study to collect information about the present policies and practices of academic libraries, in registering for loans students from other institutions. The first part of the survey sent to all academic libraries identified the regulations placed on visiting student borrowers; the second part asked for reactions to possible scenarios for the future, a future leading towards open borrowing. The questions in this part of the survey were answered on the basis of acceptable preferences; respondents eliminated all the answers that were totally unacceptable to them, and they indicated their preferences for the remainder. The report, *A National Library Card for External Students*, was published in 1987, and concluded that while a standard, nationally acceptable library card was not necessary, standardised information, procedures and undertakings were.

The report recommended that a library act as a coordinating agency, to establish and maintain conditions in which university and college libraries would permit visiting external students to borrow. Deakin University Library compiles annually a list for each State, as well as for all Australia, detailing the conditions under which libraries allow students from other institutions to borrow, the rules they impose, and details on any fees charged. Many institutions send the guide to their external students. However, the situation is still varied and confusing - to librarians as well as to students! - and greater effort at coordination is required. A fuss-free system for extending borrowing privileges to visiting student borrowers is needed; a system which is simple for the students, so it encourages them to register for loans, and also simple for the libraries, so that they can provide information to students, and statistics to each other.

User Education

Cooperative ventures in user education opportunities for off-campus students are also receiving some attention. The possibilities were explored at a national seminar in 1989, and the concept of cooperative user education was cautiously endorsed by the participants. Some institutions are beginning to work together in producing packages which can be used in any library, to introduce students to resources in a particular subject area, or show them how to use a specific reference tool. Inspired by the cooperative packages developed in Britain (Earnshaw, 1974), this will be an area that individual libraries and groups of libraries turn their attention to, in the 1990's. The production of quality user-education packages requires not only time and money, but also creative ideas; developing new and imaginative packages will be helped enormously by cooperation.

A National Forum

The Association continued its fostering of interest in distance education by hosting in 1987, a two-day forum on the coordination of support services to external students through institutional, public and other libraries. The forum was chaired by Professor Richard Johnson from the Commonwealth Tertiary Education Commission (CTEC), and at the time, Chairman of CTEC's Standing Committee on External Studies. Representatives from various sectors, as well as divisions of the Association, were invited to attend the Forum; these included the Committee of Australian University Librarians, the Association of Librarians of Colleges of Advanced Education, the Australian Advisory Council on Bibliographic Services; directors of external studies; the Australian and South Pacific External Studies Association; public libraries; special libraries and school libraries. Working papers were presented by seven speakers and these served to focus discussion on particular issues effecting the provision of library service to off-campus students. The forum concluded with the identification of six major areas of concern:

1. the need for improved coordination of information;
2. the need to define more clearly the role of libraries;
3. more effective dissemination of information;
4. access to other libraries;
5. the importance of information technology;
6. definition of the clientele.

A small working party, established to follow up on these issues, decided that more effective dissemination of information was an issue that could be dealt with quickly.

Consequently, the Special Interest Group produced for 1989 a guide, which in convenient check-list format, detailed the library services provided by institutions enrolling external students. *Library Services for External Students: A Guide* is designed to assist both librarians and

students who may not be aware of the library services offered by each
institution. The guide was distributed free of charge to all state,
special, school, TAFE and academic libraries. Publication and
distribution were made possible by donations from several academic
institutions. A 1990 edition of the guide has not been produced; given
the round of amalgamations, affiliations and associations currently
occurring in Australian higher education, production has been deferred
until 1991. At that time, it will be possible to evaluate the usefulness
of the guide, by reference to a brief questionnaire inserted in the
guide, for completion by 1990.

Conclusion

The development of external studies in Australia occurred so rapidly
in the 1970's and 1980's that librarians were often forced to be reactive
rather than proactive in the development of library services. With the
government's new rationale for higher education in Australia, there is
for the first time a national focus on cooperation and rationalisation,
that will foster discussion and collaborative ventures between the
libraries of the designated distance education centres. This will
become increasingly necessary as the Government's equity and access
policies for higher education produce more courses offered in the
external mode, and more students. One of the challenges that lies in
front of distance education centres and their libraries, is the costing of
all aspects of off-campus provision and delivery, so that true
comparisons may be made with on-campus teaching and support
services. The future is an exciting one, where, at last, a united library
voice may have a chance to provide quality library services to off-
campus students. Much work remains to be done over this coming
decade, in designing systems, monitoring and evaluating them, over a
period of change, cooperative focus, and united efforts.

References

Annual report of the university librarian for 1985. (1985). St. Lucia: University of Queensland.

Commonwealth of Australia. (1988). *Higher education: a policy statement.* Canberra: Australian Government Publishing Service.

Commonwealth Tertiary Education Commission. (1985). *Selected advanced education statistics.* Belconnen, A.C.T.: The Commission.

Crocker, C. (Ed.). (1982). *Guidelines for library services to external students.* Sydney, N.S.W.: Library Association of Australia.

Crocker, C. (1989, May). *Let's make the stranger feel at home ....* Paper presented at the national seminar on cooperative reader education ("The Stranger in the Library"), organized by the LAA University and College Libraries Section, N.S.W. Group and the Special Interest Group on Distance Education, Sydney.

Crocker, C. (1991). Off-campus library services in Australia. *Library Trends, 39*(4), 495-513.

Crocker, C., Cameron, M. & Farish, S. (1987). *A national library card for external students? An investigation into possible system borrowing privileges for all external students at all tertiary libraries.* Geelong: Deakin University.

Crocker, C. & Grimison, C. (1989). *Library services for external students: a guide.* Sydney: Library Association of Australia.

Earnshaw, F. (1974). An example of cooperative development of library use instruction programs. In Lubans, J. (Ed.), *Educating the Library User.* New York: Bowker.

Houle, C.O. (1984). *The external degree.* San Francisco: Jossey-Bass.

Johnson, R. (1983). *The provision of external studies in Australian higher education.* Canberra: Commonwealth Tertiary Education Commission.

Lessin, B.M. (Ed.). (1983). *The Off-campus Library Services Conference Proceedings.* Mt. Pleasant, MI: Central Michigan University Press.

Store, R. & Clyde, L. (1981). *Looking out from down under: A preliminary report of a survey of library services to external students in Australia and overseas.* Queensland: Townsville College of Advanced Education.

Universities Commission. (1985). *Selected university statistics.* Belconnen, A.C.T.: Universities Commission.

Weatherford, J.W. (1983). Prerequisites for campus quality library services to external degree programs. In B.M. Lessin (Ed.), *The Off-campus Library Services Conference Proceedings* (pp. 34-37). Mt. Pleasant, MI: Central Michigan University Press.

Winter, A. & Cameron, M. (1983). *External students and their libraries.* Geelong: Deakin University.

Note

[1] Ms. Crocker's paper was presented at the third Off-campus Library Services Conference, Reno, Nevada, and appeared in the 1987 edition of the conference proceedings.

Separate Library Collections for Off-campus Programs: Some Arguments For And Against[1]

Raymond K. Fisher

Introduction

In this paper I attempt to answer two related questions: (a) What factors should be taken into account by a university or college when deciding whether to set up (or maintain) a separate library collection in support of its off-campus courses? and (b) In what circumstances is it desirable to provide small deposit collections at each off-campus teaching site? The main differences between external programs, and the related library problems, are first identified, with some suggested solutions. Some existing models of library service are mentioned, with particular reference to the system of extramural libraries and bookboxes in the UK. The main arguments for and against this system are outlined, and some general conclusions are drawn.

The Different Kinds of Teaching Programs

There is clearly no single model of library service which is suitable for all external programs, and I have first tried to isolate the main differences in the various programs which exist. These differences may themselves help to establish some of the main criteria to use in making decisions about separate libraries.

1. The range and nature of the subjects taught

An external program may cover a wide range of academic subjects or concentrate on one main area of study. Or there may be various combinations between these two extremes. In addition there will be differences in the amount of emphasis on vocational/non-vocational study and on credit/non-credit work.

2. The mode of learning

This may be individualized, independent learning at home, or based on class/group teaching at an off-campus centre, or some combination of the two. This is basically a difference between distance (correspondence) education and fact-to-face tuition.

3. The size of the course program

One institution may offer hundreds of external courses and attract thousands of enrollments, while another may have only a handful of each.

4. The relationship between the external and internal programs

Some institutions offer an exact replica externally of the courses which are taught internally, while at others there is little similarity between the two.

5. The location and nature of off-campus teaching sites

Assuming a system of class teaching (see 2), there may be a large or small number of sites; some will be widely scattered and isolated geographically, others more closely grouped in urban areas; various types of premises may be used, ranging from large branch campuses to small village halls.

6. The location of students

Assuming a system of independent learning (see 2), some students may live and work a great distance from the home institution, others may be close to it.

7. The institutional basis of the program

Some universities or colleges may have a separate continuing education (or external/extramural) unit, dedicated solely to this purpose; at others the off-campus courses may be offered directly by individual subject departments.

8. The financial basis of the program

Some courses (and whole programs) may be self-financing, others highly subsidized.

The particular combination of the above elements which is found in any one off-campus teaching program will in turn determine the kind of problems to which a supporting library service should address itself. The main library-related problems which arise under each of the above headings, and suggested solutions, are as follows.

Library Problems and Suggested Solutions

1. A wide range of subjects will require a similarly wide-ranging library stock. If it is a large program (see 3 above), a university's central library should not be expected to do justice to it as well as to its internal clientele, and in this case a separate collection is desirable. A much narrower subject area, however, could be serviced direct from the central library, provided that the library stock was strengthened in that area. This would be particularly appropriate where the type of literature most often required was periodical articles, most of which might already be in the library's stock, and which could be made available in photocopied form without prejudice to the full-time students.

Some subjects, especially in the social sciences, require access to up-to-date information, and this service is more appropriately supplied by the existing central library resources.

2. A system of distance education for individual students learning at home by correspondence requires an individualized library service, the provision of materials on request dispatched to each student independently. These requests are likely to be geared closely to students' written assignments, and a separate library dedicated to this function will be more able to anticipate them and supply them when needed.

Class teaching requires a different approach, as the main characteristic here is several students learning together and so often requiring the same texts at the same time. It is in this context that the practice of small collections (consisting of the required texts and further reading), deposited in the classroom, is to be recommended (see further under "Extramural libraries" below). These collections are best provided by a separate library which can build up a stock which is specially geared to the courses which it is supporting.

There are, of course, many new teaching methods, making use of educational technology, such as computer-assisted learning, tele-conferencing, and video instruction, but most of these will continue to require the kind of conventional library services with which this paper deals.

3. A large course program means that a large proportion of the stock of a separate library is likely to be in use at any one time, thus justifying the investment in it. A separate library is not economically justifiable where the course program is small, and especially where the courses cover only a narrow subject range.

4. Where the nature of the off-campus program is very different from that offered internally, there is a good case for building up a library with a stock and function different from that of the central collection. However, where the programs, and therefore the demands, are similar, there is an equally good case for having a separate library but for the opposite reason, i.e., that a central library cannot adequately serve two different but competing student bodies from a single collection.

5. The use of a large number of different teaching centres is a common feature of external programs. Clearly it is not feasible to provide each centre with its own comprehensive library. A compromise, consisting of small collections deposited in or near the classrooms for the duration of the courses, seems to be the common-sense solution. Further arguments for this practice are mentioned under "Extramural libraries" below. A branch campus or large teaching centre, on the other hand, may well justify the provision of a permanent library on site. In both cases it would make sense if such collections were supplied from a separate extramural library.

6. It is desirable for those external students who live or work near to their home institution to have access to (and borrowing rights at) its central library. However, the proportion of these students is likely to be small, and the majority will need an off-campus library provision, as outlined above.

7. Where a university has a continuing education or external studies department, there is clearly more chance that such a unit will provide a unified library service than if external programs are fragmented among different departments. In the latter case the central library staff should be responsible for co-ordinating an off-campus library service.

8. One of the main problems in the provision of an off-campus library

service is the establishment of regular funding each year to support it.
An allocation of money specifically for this purpose is essential, and
this would seem more likely to be forthcoming where the course
program is profit-making, or at least self-financing. However, it has
been shown that subsidized programs can also generate an adequate
library service, in those cases where academic standards are a high
priority.

Some Existing Library Services

The above statements reveal the large number of variables which exist
in the whole area of off-campus education. The kind of library service
actually offered in any particular instance will depend to some extent
on local traditions and attitudes. For example, in Australia the general
pattern is individualized correspondence education with the supporting
library service coming from the institution's central library (e.g.,
Deakin University, University of New England), or, more rarely, from
a separate collection (e.g., University of Queensland). In the UK most
off-campus education is classroom teaching, usually with deposit
collections supplied by a separate extramural library; but students on
the Open University's individualized correspondence courses receive
no direct library service from that university. In the USA the range of
offerings is so wide, that it is difficult to generalize; but prominent at
each end of the spectrum is Central Michigan University's central
library service to individual students (covering a relatively narrow
subject area) and the State University System of Florida's Extension
Library Service delivering deposit collections to classes (and covering
a wide subject area). In contrast, in East European countries external
students are mainly non-attending and independent, sometimes able to
use a postal service from their university library but otherwise using
any library they can.

Extramural Libraries in the UK:
Their Contribution to the Debate

It is hoped that the factors which are most relevant in trying to answer
our two original questions are now clearer. However, they are the
kind of questions which, in any particular case, in the end have to be
answered mainly by common-sense, experience and a knowledge of
local conditions. For this reason the second part of this paper looks
at the role and function of extramural libraries in the UK with special
reference to the University of Birmingham, and at the rationale behind

their existence; and it is hoped that this "local" experience will throw light on the wider questions.

Most adult students attending off-campus classes are busy people, often with heavy occupational and domestic responsibilities. The extramural departments of universities recognize this fact, and all those universities in the UK which have a sizeable extramural responsibility have set up their own separate libraries in an attempt specifically to meet the needs of these students. The main function of an extramural library is to support the teaching program of the department of which it is a part, by the provision of books and other materials for the use of students and lecturers. The usual method of provision for off-campus students is a collection of books for each course (the "book-box"); students may borrow from this collection and it is retained at the meeting place for the duration of the course. The books provided are carefully selected by be relevant to the course, and every effort is made to have the required books available at the time when they are needed. The best of these collections include not only books but also a wide range of learning materials for students and teaching aids for staff, including off-prints, music scores, records and tapes, and maps.

The main arguments against a system of book-boxes or deposit collections are: (a) that the provision of a relatively narrow range of texts in the classroom may actually deter students from exploring their subject fully through the breadth of materials available in a library, and (b) that the amount of use of such collections is relatively low. (See further Drodge, 1984).

The main arguments in favour of this system are: (a) that much of the material in these collections is not readily available either in bookshops or in public libraries, and that the system meets resource requirements which would otherwise go unmet, and (b) that where book borrowing is low, the fault lies not in the nature of the system itself but rather in the way the book-boxes are made up, e.g., in the consultation procedures used to determine their contents and in the degree of promotion given to books in the class by the lecturer. It has already been shown (Fisher, 1986), that extramural students in the UK do proportionately as much reading as their internal counterparts.

The Opinions of the Lecturers

But perhaps the most persuasive arguments in favour of the book-box system come from the teachers. There is clear evidence that in many cases such collections are the "life-blood" of a class, and that academic standards suffer if an adequate collection is not provided. This evidence consists mainly of statements made by lecturers in their course reports, and the following extracts are quoted from some of the reports at Birmingham University for the session 1985-86:

1. Course "The castles of the Southern Marches" in Leominster (Herefordshire): "Books and photocopied material well read - especially valuable for students living some distance from a good library."

2. Course "New light on the Dark Ages" in Sutton Coldfield: "The books have been used extensively and are clearly a popular provision."

3. Course "History of British landscape painting" in Ledbury (Herefordshire): "Reading centered on the period or artist covered weekly and books were used in class quite frequently, as well as borrowed."

4. Course "Women novelists--from Jane Austen to Margaret Drabble" in Broadway (Worcestershire). "Everyone read all the texts and some a lot more besides, either from the book-box or through their local libraries."

5. Course "Worcestershire local history from original records" in Worcester: "I was very pleased with the way the students made full use of the book-box for background reading and in conjunction with the documents being studied."

6. Course "Voices in literature--the 1950s" in Kemerton (Worcestershire): "Excellent use was made of the books supplied for a structured reading program."

7. Course "Israelite religion" in Birmingham: "Equipment and books were adequate, although of some basic books several copies would have been useful."

8. Course "Faraway places" (literature) in Malvern: "It was not easy to get the books read with six copies and a class of twenty."

9. Course "Beethoven's string quartets" in Birmingham. "Good book

supply, although we could always do with more scores which we use all the time and have to share a lot."

10. Course "The historical background to the life of Jesus" in Birmingham: "The copies of Josephus *Antiquities* arrived too late to be of much use on the course, and more copies of the Penguin Josephus would have been useful; otherwise the book supply was fine."

The last four of these statements are critical of the book-supply, in the sense that not enough was provided, or it was supplied too late; but these criticisms are themselves implicitly supportive of this kind of service as an essential feature of off-campus teaching.

It should be noted that all the above were "liberal" adult education courses (not leading to named awards) with the exception of (7), which was a component in the part-time degree curriculum. The degree courses tend to make even greater demands on the book-box service than do the liberal courses because of the difficulties of access to the central library.

Further Arguments for Separateness

The raison d'etre of an extramural department is to take the scholarship and resources of the university to the general public, and a library which "takes the books to the students" is seen to be a crucial part of this process. The question whether (in the UK context) this service comes best from a central or from a separate library may have already been answered implicitly in the above statements, but it requires further elaboration.

A separate library makes most sense where there is a large program of courses, a wide range of subjects and a fairly large geographical spread of class centers. For it can build up and circulate specialized collections to meet a multiplicity of demand in a way which neither a university central library nor public libraries can do without prejudice to other users. It can also satisfy the need to commit book stock and other materials to a class for up to nine months at a time. In addition, the staff of a dedicated library can more easily establish close contact with the class lecturers at an early stage and keep in touch with them as courses proceed in order to meet new demands.

The Question of Multiple Copies: A Birmingham Survey

Another essential feature of a separate library for off-campus courses is the holding of multiple copies of standard works. These are both for simultaneous distribution to different classes and also for simultaneous reading by students on the same course. This is not normally a feature of a university central library. In order to establish the actual difference in this respect, in quantitative terms, between the central library and the extramural library at the University of Birmingham, a small survey was carried out in early 1986. One aim was to discover the extent of duplication between the two libraries, but the main aim was to find out how many more copies, on average, of any one title were held by the extramural library than by the central library. A sample of book-lists, covering all the main subject areas, were taken from the 1983-84 off-campus courses and checked against both catalogues (the two-year time gap allowed for all recent purchases to appear in the main library's catalogue). The results were as follows:

1. Total number of titles on a sample of extramural booklists: 642 = 100%

2. Number of these titles held by University Library (UL): 448 = 69.78%

3. Number of these titles held by Extramural Library (EML): 538 = 83.8%

4. Multiples:
   (a) No. of titles of which 2 or more copies in EML: 372 = 69.14% of total held in EML

   (b) No. of titles of which 2 or more copies in UL: 100 = 22.32% of total held in UL

   (c) No. of (multiple) copies of EML's 372 multiple titles: 2458 average no. of copies in multiple set = 6.61 (2458/372)

   (d) No. of copies of UL's 100 multiple titles: 256 average no. of copies in multiple set = 2.56 (256/100)

   (e) No. of UL titles available only on short loan: 42 = 9.37% of total titles held.

The main conclusions to be drawn from this are:

1. A relatively high proportion (nearly 70%) of extramural-type books are held by the main library. This finding supports the arguments for a separate library, as it indicates that there would be undue pressures on the same titles if the central library were the only service. Nearly 10% of the titles in the main library are already under undue pressure, as they are in the short loan collection.

2. The extramural library possesses far more multiple copies of titles than does the main library. In the latter there are two or more copies of only 22% of titles while the equivalent figure for the former is 69%. In addition, the extramural library's holdings of music study scores were checked against those of the university's music library, and it was found that the average number of copies of any one score was ten in the extramural and two in the music library. These findings substantiate the statement above about the importance of multiple copies in a service to off-campus classes, and also provide justification for the decision at Birmingham to maintain a separate extramural library and to continue to supply off-campus deposit collections.

Conclusions

In this paper I have not touched on some of the major problems connected with off-campus library services, such as bibliographic instruction, access to catalogues, literature searching, and the possible use of technology such as telefacsimile. As our primary objective is to enable our students, in what is often a difficult off-campus situation, to study and learn as effectively as possible, we should aim to take materials and information to the students, and the above aspects can be incorporated in any system which is adopted (whether central or separate) with that aim in mind. This paper is based on the philosophy that the main value of a library lies in the service which it can supply immediately rather than in the back up service to which it can give access.

It is therefore with this principle of immediacy in mind that the pros and cons of separate libraries and of deposit collections have been considered in this paper, and should be considered in any local context. However, the range of variables in course programs outlined above indicates that "separateness" may not always be the best solution. In describing the system generally adopted in the UK for extramural programs, and the reasons behind it, I hope that I have identified the main factors which should be considered by others in the evaluation of other systems elsewhere.

Updating Addendum

The main aim of the original paper was to establish some criteria for making decisions about separate or integrated library services and about the provision of deposit collections at off-campus sites. The factors involved in establishing these criteria are fairly general and remain largely unchanged. However, since the paper was first written four years ago, some changes have occurred in the UK relating to extramural libraries (described in the second part of the paper as an example of an existing type of service). These changes are noted here, as they affect the nature of these libraries' "contribution to the debate."

The role of university departments of extramural studies in the UK has been slowly changing in recent years. Many are now called department of continuing and/or adult education, with an increasing emphasis on the provision of courses on-campus and with the main expansion in the field of award-bearing courses and vocational training. The off-campus programmes, which are almost entirely "liberal" (non-credit) adult education, have therefore remained fairly static, or in some cases have decreased, in size. In turn, extramural librarians have been looking increasingly at their on-campus role, at their relationship with university main libraries, and at the possibility of special joint provision for part-time adult students on campus.

To this extent the "separateness" of extramural libraries is being slightly watered down, and this trend may continue, with the government's emphasis on widening access to higher education (involving larger numbers of part-time and mature students).   However, their separateness is still a distinctive feature, and the comments in the original paper about the nature of their service still apply.   In particular, their holding of multiple copies of texts for class use, (i.e., literary texts, standard works, textbooks, music scores, etc.), has been shown by a recent survey at Birmingham (Fisher, 1989) to be of greater importance (for serving the needs of students) than previously thought.

It is to be hoped that the current emphasis on new part-time degree programmes on-campus will be extended to off-campus sites during the

next few years. If this happens, then all the factors listed in the
original paper, together with the role of information technology, will
need to be considered by each university, in deciding which type of
library service it will offer.

References

Drodge, S. (1984). *Adult education library provision*. Leicester: East
Midlands Branch of the Library Association.

Fisher, R.K. (1989).   Library services for extramural courses: the
results of a survey, University of Birmingham, 1987. *Studies in the
Education of Adults*, *21*(1), 57-64.

Fisher, R.K. (1986).   Off-campus students and reading. In B.M. Lessin
(Ed.), *The Off-Campus Library Services Conference Proceedings*
(pp. 49-59). Mt. Pleasant, MI: Central Michigan University Press.

Note

[1] Mr. Fisher's paper was presented at the third Off-campus Library
Services Conference, Reno, Nevada, and appeared in the 1987 edition
of the conference proceedings.

Thirteen Key Ingredients in Off-Campus Library Services: A Canadian Perspective[1]

Alexander L. Slade

What are some of the key ingredients in an off-campus library service? Can these ingredients be used as standards of comparison? This paper will discuss how these questions were addressed by a group of distance education librarians in British Columbia.

Background

The literature on off-campus library services in Canada to 1985 was relatively sparse. Three papers published between 1976 and 1980 are worthy of note: Wiseman (1976), Orton and Wiseman (1977), and Mount and Turple (1980). The papers by Wiseman and Orton and Wiseman discuss a survey shared by Queen's University and Trent University in 1975. While both papers focus on the issues of local library support and on-site collections, recommendations are made regarding professional support from the university library, bibliographic instruction, and a "hot line" telephone service. The article by Mount and Turple describes a model off-campus library service established at Laurentian University. In addition to supplying on-site collections, the library offers service to individual students, including telephone access, bibliographic assistance and provision of material by mail.

In British Columbia (B.C.), the four major post-secondary institutions, the University of British Columbia, the University of Victoria, Simon Fraser University and the Open Learning Institute, offer comprehensive library services to their off-campus students. The model of service present in British Columbia is, in many ways, similar to the model at Laurentian University (Mount and Turple, 1980). The librarians responsible for off-campus library services in B.C. meet periodically to discuss matters of mutual concern. At one of those meetings in 1983, it was suggested that, since the Canadian literature on this area of library service is so limited, an effort should be made to discover what other university libraries across the country are doing for their students at a distance. To this end, the four B.C. librarians composed a letter (Appendix A) to inquire about off-campus library services and sent it to the library directors at Canadian universities which have extension programs. In total, forty-two letters were sent and thirty-one replies were received (a 74% response rate).

The question facing the B.C. librarians at that point was what to do with the information received. No definite plan had been formulated ahead of time because of the uncertainty regarding the type of replies which would be received. As it turned out, some respondents gave detailed descriptions of their off-campus library services. Twenty libraries out of the thirty-one (65%) which replied to the letter reported that they are involved in one or more areas of service to their students at a distance. Other libraries admitted they were not currently active in any area. A few institutions indicated there was a need for their libraries to become more involved in offering these services. Several respondents expressed interest in receiving information about the off-campus library services in British Columbia.

The replies to the letter of inquiry inspired the B.C. librarians to undertake three other projects to promote awareness of off-campus library services in Canada. The first was to propose to the Canadian Library Association that a workshop on this topic be held at the annual conference in Calgary, Alberta, in June of 1985. That proposal was accepted. The second was to write a paper describing off-campus library services in British Columbia (Slade, Whitehead, Piovesan, & Webb, 1987). The third project was to classify and compare the information received from the other Canadian libraries.

Classification of Services

At present, Canada does not have any licensing boards or accrediting bodies, nor any statutes, regulations, or standards for off-campus programs as described by Lessin (1982). Canada also lacks any guidelines for off-campus library service endorsed by a provincial or national library association. The ACRL "Guidelines for Extended Campus Library Service" (Association of College and Research Libraries, 1982) are not formally recognized in Canada and only one of the respondents to the B.C. librarians' letter acknowledged the existence of these guidelines.

It became apparent that each institution in the country had independently developed its own response to the issue of library support for its off-campus and distance education students. In the replies from those universities which do offer some form of library support, a number of common elements of service were evident. The B.C. librarians decided to classify these "ingredients" of service as they emerged from the letters. Using the B.C. services as models and analyzing the information contained in the letters, the librarians established a list of thirteen categories to reflect the types of services offered (Appendix B).

The B.C. librarians realized that the list of thirteen categories or the survey form, as it was eventually labelled, was not a sophisticated or scientific instrument to measure the quality of the different library services. It did not probe into areas such as university-approved policy statements, finances and facilities as contained in the unapproved Review Guide prepared by the ACRL Standards and Accreditation Committee (Hodowanec, 1983). In addition, it did not attempt to deal with four major variables which influence the nature of an off-campus library service: the number of courses or programs offered and their enrollments; the mode of course delivery (face-to-face instruction in specified locations versus instruction by distance education methods such as correspondence and educational television); the proximity of the students to the main library and to other major research collections; and the technology available to the main library for use at off-campus locations (e.g., online catalogs). However, these topics were not emphasized by the respondents in any consistent way.

The B.C. letter asked about services offered to off-campus students and the list of categories reflected what the different libraries chose to tell about their operations. It was felt that distribution of a more elaborate and probing questionnaire would alienate more respondents than it would produce useful results. This suspicion was confirmed when completed survey forms (See Appendix B) were sent to nineteen of the respondents asking them to confirm the affirmative and negative responses in each category and to provide more information if appropriate. Seventeen libraries (89%) returned their annotated survey forms.

Following is a discussion of each of the thirteen categories used to classify the information on Canadian off-campus library services. In addition to reporting on the affirmative response rate from Canadian libraries, the commentary attempts to indicate the significance of each category or "ingredient" as a component in an off-campus library service. In cases where an area has been well discussed or documented in the literature, the remarks on significance have been minimized.

1. Core Collections

A core collection refers to a collection of library material placed on-site for an off-campus course or program. The first category was used to identify those libraries which respond to requests from faculty or administration to send books, articles and other material to course sites.

The issues of core collections and arrangements with local libraries appear frequently in the literature on off-campus library services (e.g., Orton and Wiseman, 1977; Mount and Turple, 1980). The provision of core collections is possibly the most traditional way in which library support is offered to off-campus face-to-face courses. This, of course, ceases to be relevant when courses are delivered by distance education methods such as correspondence and educational television and students are scattered over a wide geographical area. Essentially, the core collection service is an extension of the on-campus reserve function. If a library is prepared to provide this service, it is demonstrating a basic level of responsibility to off-campus education by making reserve material available to students regardless of location.

The B.C. librarians found that, among the responding libraries, most were willing to supply core collections on request for off-campus face-to-face courses, provided that the course was held far enough away from the campus to make commuting to the main library impractical. In some cases, special funding had to be found to purchase materials for a core collection, but in most cases the willingness of the library to cooperate in this area was confirmed. Sixteen (52%) of the respondents indicated they are presently active in providing this service. Some respondents provided more information in this area than others, but, on examination, there were not enough consistent details to warrant subdividing the category into more specific topics such as contractual arrangements with other libraries and the existence of separate extension libraries within the main library.

2. Specific Requests

This category represents one of the cornerstones in an off-campus library service. Is the library willing to send specifically identified material to an individual off-campus student in response to a request received by mail, telephone or some form of electronic data transmission? An affirmative response implies that the library has assumed a degree of responsibility for supporting off-campus education and for meeting the information needs of individual students. With the resources of the main library available by mail (or by some other means of delivery), instructors no longer have to limit readings and assignments to material which is locally available. In addition, off-campus students can have more flexibility in choosing resources for assignments, together with the option of pursuing a topic in greater depth than would normally be possible were they entirely dependent on core collections and local library holdings.

Seventeen (55%) of the libraries which responded to the letter of inquiry indicated that they do attempt to supply specific material to individual off-campus students.

3. Reference Queries

This category represents another cornerstone in an off-campus library service. Is the library willing to answer reference questions and conduct subject searches for off-campus students? Many off-campus students do not have access to appropriate bibliographies and indexes in their local libraries. Core collections are limited in the amount of information they can provide for individual essay topics and assignments. By providing a means for off-campus faculty to set appropriate assignments and for off-campus students to obtain information to complete those assignments, the library is confirming its responsibility in supporting the concept of quality in off-campus academic programs as discussed by authors such as McCabe (1983).

Fifteen (48%) of the Canadian respondents acknowledged that they do provide some form of reference service on request for their students at a distance. Curiously, one library replied that it would answer reference questions from off-campus students, but would not conduct subject searches for them.

4. Special Telephone Line

The category for a special telephone line was based on the model of service present in British Columbia rather than on information extracted from the respondents' letters. The focal point of all four library services in B.C. is a special telephone line to the library for off-campus students to use to request material and information for their courses. The four telephone services in B.C. have the following features in common: students are advised through publicity to call collect; the lines operate twenty-four hours a day; telephone answering machines are used to accept collect calls and record information and requests.

As emphasized by authors such as McCabe (1983), Rumery (1983) and Johnson (1984), the telephone is the off-campus student's link to the library and serves as a substitute for the student being able to walk into the building in person to select his/her own material. It is traditional for on-campus students to have free, convenient access to the resources of the academic library. A toll-free telephone line is a means to provide the off-campus student with an equitable form of library access. The availability of such a line implies that the institution has recognized the value of library access to off-campus education.

In this survey, the B.C. librarians looked for other libraries which utilized a similar concept of phone service. Five libraries (16% of the respondents) indicated that they had toll-free telephone lines available for their off-campus students.

5. Advertisement of Services

This category is very significant for off-campus library services because it is a reflection of whether a service has become institutionalized. For a library to advertise its off-campus service implies that the service has gained acceptance from the administration. The implications extend further to the areas of funding, staff, and resources. By publicizing the availability of a service, the library is indicating that it is prepared to respond to a demand for that service within established parameters.

In the replies to the B.C. letter, several libraries reported that they did provide some services to their off-campus students on an ad hoc basis but, for various reasons, did not formally advertise or publicize these services. Twelve libraries (39% of the respondents) indicated that they did advertise their services.

6. Librarian

Another significant indicator of the institutionalization of an off-campus library service is whether at least one librarian has either full-time or part-time responsibility for the service as part of his/her job description. For a library to devote the time of a member of the professional staff to this service implies a high level of commitment to off-campus programs. Most university libraries in Canada do not have a person designated as an "extension librarian" or, a librarian with a similar title. In general, off-campus activities are inserted into the schedules of librarians whose primary responsibilities lie in other areas. Only six libraries (19%) responded that they had a librarian on staff with off-campus services as a primary component of his/her job description.

7. Support Staff

Many of the functions associated with an off-campus library service can be performed at a clerical or library assistant level. These functions include retrieving material from the library collections, charging out books, photocopying, typing labels and reply forms, and record keeping. Established off-campus services should have at least one person to perform these tasks as part of their job description. The person may be full-time, part-time, or sessional. Eleven Canadian libraries (35%) replied that they had such a position on staff. It was of interest to note that two of those eleven libraries had a member of the support staff coordinating the off-campus service in place of a librarian.

8. Bibliographic Instruction

The relevance of bibliographic instruction in an off-campus library service has been adequately discussed by other authors (e.g., Brown, 1983; Peyton, 1983). In this context, several forms of instruction can be utilized, including personal visits by librarians to course sites, audio-visual presentations, teleconferencing, computer-assisted instruction, and written instruction. Materials for instruction can include on-site reference collections, microfiche and online catalogs, facilities for online literature searches, the resources of local libraries, and prepared instructional packages.

Eight libraries in Canada (26%) replied that they are currently involved in some form of bibliographic instruction for off-campus courses. The most common form mentioned by the respondents was personal visits to course sites.

9. Online Bibliographic Services

The use of computerized literature searching in off-campus library services has been well documented in the literature (Weinstein and Strasser, 1983; Cookingham, 1983; Rumery, 1983; Ream and Weston, 1983). There are several advantages to using online searching in this context. One major benefit is that it saves time for the library staff, reducing the need to conduct manual literature searches for off-campus students. Another major advantage is that it usually gives the student more involvement in defining and limiting a topic and in selecting his/her own references. Depending on the organization of the services, online searching can also save time for the student and give faculty more flexibility in setting assignments.

In Canada, at present, most computerized searching for off-campus students is done by librarians at the campus library. The student requests information from the library by letter or phone, the search is conducted at the librarian's convenience, and the results are mailed to the student. Usually there is a charge for this service. In some cases, a librarian will initiate an online search on behalf of a student as an alternative to conducting a manual literature search for this user. In these instances, the student is usually not charged for the search. Twelve respondents (39%) indicated that their library would conduct, on request, a computerized literature search for an off-campus student.

10. Interlibrary Loans

This category was used to establish which libraries would initiate interlibrary loan requests on behalf of their off-campus students. As in category 4 (special telephone line), this section was modeled on the British Columbia services. In B.C., the campus library assumes primary responsibility for providing material to its off-campus users. Students are not expected to request interlibrary loans through a local library. Instead, the students are encouraged to make their requests through the telephone service to the campus library which in turn will initiate, if appropriate, an interlibrary loan request on behalf of the student. The librarians initially screen these requests to determine if another item could be substituted and, if not, if there is sufficient time to obtain the material from another library.

Since interlibrary loans are a traditional on-campus service, some means should be available to off-campus students to obtain specific items not held by the home library. This is based on the assumption that a comprehensive off-campus service assumes full responsibility for meeting the library needs of its users and attempts to provide services comparable to those available on-campus. Nine Canadian libraries (29%) replied that they do initiate interlibrary loan requests for their off-campus users.

11. Charges for Service

The objective of this category was to learn how many libraries provide off-campus library services free-of-charge to the user and, inversely, how many hold the user responsible for some of the costs of service. There are two significant rationales for an institution to offer off-campus library services at no charge. First, the services are essentially a form of compensation to the student for being unable to use the resources of the main library in person. If the objective of an off-campus library service is to enhance the quality of academic programs (McCabe, 1983), a system of charges would be to the detriment of this concept of quality since it would likely discourage library use amongst students who are already at a disadvantage in this regard. A second rationale for free services is to minimize the complications and staff time in record-keeping and fee-collecting.

Among the respondents, thirteen libraries (42%) indicated that, with the exception of computerized literature search fees, they provide their off-campus service at no cost to the student. Seven libraries (23%) reported that their students are responsible for the cost of photocopying or postage or both. None of the libraries reported that they charge basic service fees or fees for loans or manual literature searches.

12. Needs Assessments

The category for needs assessments was created to discover which libraries take an active role in planning services geared to the needs of the institution's off-campus courses and programs. This implies that library staff meet with the relevant campus educators and administrators to determine how the library can assist in developing and providing resources for off-campus courses and how the students can effectively obtain information for their assignments and projects. In some cases, the library may need to promote its off-campus services in order to achieve the desired result and to enhance the quality of the course or program in question. A library's active involvement in this area tends to reflect a high level of institutional commitment to off-campus service.

Eleven libraries (35%) which responded to the B.C. letter and returned the completed survey form acknowledged that they undertake formal or informal needs assessments for off-campus courses and programs and use this information to plan library services.

13. Evaluation

The premise of this category is that the library staff periodically review the services and resources available to off-campus students and faculty and evaluate their effectiveness. As in the previous category (needs assessment), a library's involvement in this area tends to indicate a high level of institutional commitment to off-campus service. Several examples and discussions of evaluation in off-campus programs can be found in the literature (e.g., Kim and Rogers, 1983; Hodowanec, 1983; Johnson, 1984).

After this category was established, the B.C. librarians realized that it was inappropriate to assume that the library staff had to conduct the evaluations. At the University of Victoria and at two other institutions which responded to the letter of inquiry, off-campus library services are evaluated as part of larger evaluation projects conducted by the campus agencies responsible for the courses or programs. In these cases, the library has input into the content of the library section of the questionnaire or project. This approach to evaluation is significant because it indicates cooperation between the library and other campus departments. By including adequate library representation in an off-campus evaluation project, the evaluator is acknowledging the importance of the library's role in the academic programs which are under review.

Including the two libraries mentioned above, thirteen Canadian libraries (42% of the respondents) reported that they are involved to some extent in the evaluation of their off-campus services.

Comparison of Services

In order to display and compare the information in the thirteen categories, the Multiplan™ software package was used on a personal computer. Originally, all respondents to the B.C. letter were listed on the spread-sheet, including those libraries which were not involved in providing any off-campus services. For the purpose of this paper, two revised versions of the spread-sheet were produced. The first version (Appendix C) lists only those libraries which have an affirmative answer for at least one of the thirteen categories. For the purposes of comparison, the four B.C. institutions were added to the spread-sheet. With the inclusion of the B.C. services, the totals on the spread-sheet will be slightly higher than those cited under the different categories in the previous section of this paper.

In Appendix C, a "1" is assigned for each "yes" answer and a "O" is assigned for each "no." This provides a maximum total of 13 for each library. These totals are displayed in the far right column of the spread-sheet. At a glance, it is possible to see by these totals which libraries are most actively involved in off-campus services. Since a few institutions offer courses entirely by distance education delivery methods (e.g., the Open Learning Institute, Athabasca University), a "O" under the core collection category does not imply that these institutions are any less active than universities which have a "1" in this category. Therefore the totals in the right-hand column should be viewed within a range (e.g., 12-13) rather than assuming that an institution with a 13 is more active than an institution with a 12. At the bottom of the spread-sheet are the totals by category, which enables the reader to see how many institutions are involved in any of the thirteen categories.

Since Appendix C is a very basic comparison of categories, another spread-sheet (Appendix D) was produced with values attached to affirmative responses in the various categories. The rationale behind this approach was that the categories reflect different levels of library involvement in off-campus services and higher values can serve as a way to give credit to libraries which go beyond offering the basic services (categories 1-3).

In Appendix D, the following values were assigned to the affirmative responses:

Categories	Values
1-3	1
4-11	2
12-13	3

The maximum total for any institution on this spread-sheet would be 25 (right-hand column). Once again, due to variations in the number and types of courses offered, availability of technology, geographic area involved, and other local conditions, it would not be fair to regard the ratings as hierarchically superior to one another. As with the spread-sheet in Appendix C, the right-hand totals should be regarded within ranges as indications of a library's involvement in off-campus services (e.g. 25-22: high level of involvement; 21-15: very active; 14-6: active; 5-0: low level of involvement).

Categories 1-3 were considered to represent basic services and had a high affirmative response rate from Canadian libraries. Categories 4-11 could have been subdivided depending on one's view of the importance of a particular category, but for the sake of simplicity, were grouped together as a second level of support indicative of a considerable degree of institutional commitment to off-campus library services. As a note of clarification, category 11 (charges for service) excludes charges for computerized literature searches since very few libraries are willing to subsidize this service to either their on-campus or off-campus students. The highest values were reserved for categories 12 and 13 (needs assessment and evaluation) since these areas are considered to be reflective of a proactive approach to off-campus library services. In this context, "proactive" implies the opposite of "reactive" and indicates the library takes initiative in planning and providing services and resources which can contribute to the quality of an off-campus academic program.

Appendix E presents a comparison of the institutional totals from the previous two appendices arranged in hierarchical order. This summary enables the reader to see the two sets of totals side by side as an indication of how the ratings are affected by the assignment of different values to different categories. It is interesting to note that the ranked order of the institutions does not change dramatically with the second set of values. These values tend to "fine-tune" the rating scheme more than they significantly alter any position on the spreadsheet.

The values assigned to the categories in Appendix D and summarized in Appendix E are arbitrary and primarily serve as an example of one approach to comparing off-campus library services. For the B.C. librarians, this approach provided a rough picture of the state of these services in Canada. This picture is being shared in the hope that other librarians will be inspired to devise their own categories to describe and compare key ingredients in this type of service and to develop an appropriate rating scheme which will reflect an institution's level of involvement in and commitment to off-campus library services.

Addendum

The decision to undertake a second survey of off-campus services in Canada was made at the initial meeting of the Canadian Library Association Interest Group on Library Services for Distance Learning in June 1987. Since the data from the first survey was released in 1985, there has been more attention devoted to this area of librarianship in publications, workshops, and conferences. In order to assess the impact of this attention on the services offered by academic libraries across the country, the members of the Interest Group decided that another survey would be useful. Because many college librarians had expressed an interest in this area, it was also decided to include Canadian colleges in the second survey distribution.

In January, 1988, a questionnaire on off-campus library services was sent to 199 post-secondary institutions in Canada: fifty-five universities and 144 colleges and technical institutes (Slade, 1988). The questionnaire was designed to determine the level of library support provided for off-campus students who are not able to visit the main or branch libraries on a regular basis.

The response rate to the questionnaire was 60%: 78% for universities and 53% for colleges. Quebec and Ontario had the lowest response rates at 22% and 63% respectively. All the other provinces had close to a 100% response rate.

Of the institutions which responded to the questionnaire, 86% of the universities and 60% of the colleges indicated that they offer off-campus or distance education courses. Of those institutions, 95% of the universities and 85% of the colleges provide some level of library support for their off-campus students.

One of the objectives of the current survey was to determine whether the universities which responded to the 1984/85 survey (discussed above) had altered their library services to off-campus students in the intervening three years. In order to compare services, the basic questions in the first thirteen categories were kept identical to those used in the earlier survey. When institutional responses from the two surveys were compared, it was found that 38% of the twenty-four universities represented in the first survey had increased their level of library support for off-campus programs, 33% had maintained the same level of support, and 21% had decreased the level of support. No reasons were apparent for these changes.

The questionnaire for the current survey was divided into fifteen categories. The two new categories represented the areas of funding and curriculum development. In each category, there was one basic question requiring a "yes" or "no" response, plus a number of secondary questions to probe for additional information. An institution qualified as providing some level of off-campus library support if it responded "yes" to any one of the fifteen basic questions. The average number of "yes" responses was nine for universities and seven for colleges, indicating that many institutions are active in several areas of off-campus library services.

For both types of institutions, the categories which had the highest affirmative response rate were those which pertained to the provision of library material for off-campus students. Over 80% of the universities and over 70% of the colleges with some level of off-campus library support reported that they are prepared to supply specific library items, answer reference questions, and conduct subject searches for off-campus students. In addition, over 80% of the universities and over 60% of the colleges indicated that they will provide core collections for off-campus courses on request.

For the purposes of this survey, a basic library outreach service exists when an institution advertises that it will send specific monographs and articles to off-campus students and will conduct literature searches for these students on request. Based on this criteria, 71% of the universities and 46% of the colleges which have some level of off-campus library support qualify as having an established outreach service. Of the institutions which do not have a library outreach service, 90% of the universities and 62% of the colleges supply core collections to off-campus sites. This data indicates that library outreach services and core collection services are the two primary means of off-campus library support in Canada. 97% of the universities and 79% of the colleges with some level of off-campus library support have either one service or the other or both.

The categories which received the lowest affirmative response rate from both universities and colleges were those which dealt with the planning and administration of off-campus library services. Less than 50% of the universities and less than 30% of the colleges with some level of off-campus library support indicated that the Library conducts needs assessments, has separate funding procedures, and is involved in curriculum development for off-campus courses. Responses to the secondary questions in these categories indicate that several institutions tend to provide off-campus library support on an ad hoc basis.

In order to compare the levels of off-campus library support provided by the different institutions, two measurements were created especially for the survey data. One measurement has been entitled the Off-Campus Library Services Index. This is a composite score combining the number of affirmative responses to the fifteen basic questions with a ranking system representing the volume of material supplied to off-campus courses and students. The other measurement has been entitled the Item/Student Ratio. This ratio is derived by dividing the total off-campus enrollment into the total number of library items supplied to off-campus students.

These two measurements provide an approximate picture of an institution's activity level in off-campus library services. Based on the Off-Campus Library Services Index, only 14% of the universities and 15% of the colleges can be categorized as having a high level of involvement in this area. Based on the Item/Student Ratio, only 30% of the universities and 15% of the colleges serve a third or more of the off-campus student population. This indicates that while many institutions have outreach services and/or core collection services and are willing to support their off-campus students, relatively few of them are supplying large quantities of library material. The enrollment statistics provided by the various institutions confirm that, on the whole, a small proportion of the off-campus students are taking advantage of the library services available to them. Further research is required to determine the reasons for this inconsistency.

References

Association of College and Research Libraries. Standards and Accreditation Committee. (1982). Guidelines for extended campus library services. *College and Research Libraries News, 43*, 86-88.

Brown, K. (1983). A bibliographic instruction model for reaching adult part-time students. In B.M. Lessin (Ed.), *The Off-campus Library Services Conference Proceedings* (pp. 169-173). Mt. Pleasant, MI: Central Michigan University Press.

Cookingham, R.M. (1983). Delivering off-campus library services in Northern California. In B.M. Lessin (Ed.), *The Off-campus Library Services Conference Proceedings* (pp. 146-154). Mt. Pleasant, MI: Central Michigan University Press.

Hodowanec, G.V. (1983). Review and revision: The preparation of "Guidelines for extended campus library services." In B.M. Lessin (Ed.), *The Off-campus Library Services Conference Proceedings* (pp. 201-210). Mt. Pleasant, MI: Central Michigan University Press.

Johnson, J.S. (1984). The Wyoming experience with the ACRL "Guidelines for extended campus library services." *College and Research Libraries News, 45,* 76-78.

Kim, M.T. & Rogers, A.R. (1983). Libraries for librarians: Identifying and evaluating resources for off-campus graduate programs in library science. In B.M. Lessin (Ed.), *The Off-campus Library Services Conference Proceedings* (pp. 190-200). Mt. Pleasant, MI: Central Michigan University Press.

Lessin, B.M. (1982). Libraries and licensure: A preliminary study of the statutes, regulations, standards, and guidelines used in the evaluation of off-campus out-of-state academic library programs. *Proceedings of the Fifth Annual Conference on Quality in Off-campus Credit Programs. Issues in Higher Education, 8,* (pp. 211-231).

McCabe, G.B. (1983). As if they were here: Library service for off-campus students. In B.M. Lessin (Ed.), *The Off-campus Library Services Conference Proceedings* (pp. 15-26). Mt. Pleasant, MI: Central Michigan University Press.

Mount, J. & Turple, J. (1980). University library service for off-campus students. *Canadian Library Journal, 37,* 47-50.

Orton, L. & Wiseman, J. (1977). Library service to part-time students. *Canadian Library Journal, 34,* 23-27.

Peyton, J.L. (1983). Bibliographic instruction at off-campus sites. In B.M. Lessin (Ed.), *The Off-campus Library Services Conference Proceedings* (pp. 174-181). Mt. Pleasant, MI: Central Michigan University Press.

Ream, J. & Weston, N. (1983). The effects of innovative extended library services on total library operations. In B.M. Lessin (Ed.), *The Off-campus Library Services Conference Proceedings* (pp. 129-137). Mt. Pleasant, MI: Central Michigan University Press.

Rumery, J.V. (1983). Decreasing the distance: The library, off-campus education and technology. In B.M. Lessin (Ed.), *The Off-campus Library Services Conference Proceedings* (pp. 51-58). Mt. Pleasant, MI: Central Michigan University Press.

Slade, A. L. (1988). *The second Canadian off-campus library services survey, 1988: Final report.* Victoria, B.C.: University of Victoria Library. (ERIC Document Reproduction Service No. ED 305 074)

Slade, A. L., Whitehead, M., Piovesan, W. & Webb, B. (1987). The evolution of library services for off-campus and distance education students in British Columbia. *PNLA Quarterly, 51* (2), 34-38.

Weinstein, G. & Strasser, D. (1983). National College of Education's extended campus library services: A model program. In B.M. Lessin (Ed.), *The Off-campus Library Services Conference Proceedings* (pp. 169-173). Mt. Pleasant, MI: Central Michigan University Press.

Wiseman, J.A. (1976). *Library service to part-time students at Trent University. A study.* (ERIC Document Reproduction Service No.

ED 157 501)

Note

¹ Mr. Slade's paper was presented at the second Off-campus Library Services Conference, Knoxville, Tennessee, and appeared in the 1987 edition of the conference proceedings.

Appendix A

B.C. *Letter of Inquiry*

Dear

We represent an informal group of distance education librarians in British Columbia who are interested in learning what our counterparts are doing in other Canadian universities. At our respective institutions we offer comprehensive library services for our students who take credit courses or do independent studies off-campus. These services include the availability of toll-free telephone lines to the university libraries, the provision of monographs and photocopied periodical articles by mail to individual students, and bibliographic assistance for reference questions. Two members of our group also supply core collections to the sites where extension courses are taught.

We are interested in knowing which other university libraries offer services similar to ours. If there is an individual in your library who acts as an extension librarian, we would appreciate this person contacting us and sending a description of the services offered to your off-campus students. In return, we will be pleased to provide information about the off-campus library services offered by the following four institutions in British Columbia: Simon Fraser University, the University of British Columbia, the Open Learning Institute and the University of Victoria.

Our purpose for initiating this contact is to collect and share information about off-campus library services on a national basis. Any assistance you can offer in putting us in touch with people operating in this area would be appreciated.

For mailing purposes, please address all correspondence to Sandy Slade at the University of Victoria Library. Thank you.

Yours sincerely,

Alexander (Sandy) Slade
Extension Librarian
University of Victoria

Barbara Webb
Student Services Librarian
Open Learning Institute

Appendix B

Canadian Off-campus Library Services Survey

INSTITUTION: _____

Please respond "yes" or "no" to each of the following statements.

1. CORE COLLECTIONS:

A collection of books and articles is sent on request to the site of an off-campus course. _____

2. SPECIFIC REQUESTS:

The library staff sends specific material to off-campus students in response to requests received by mail or telephone. _____

3. REFERENCE QUERIES:

The library staff answers reference questions and conducts subject searches for off-campus students in response to requests received by mail or telephone. _____

4. SPECIAL TELEPHONE LINE:

The library has a special "toll-free" telephone line for off-campus students to request library material. (Note: "toll-free" can be interpreted to mean that the library accepts collect calls.) _____

5. ADVERTISEMENT OF SERVICES:

Library services for off-campus students are publicized in brochures, handbooks, and other literature which is available to all off-campus faculty and students. _____

6. LIBRARIAN:

At least one librarian has either full-time or part-time responsibilities for off-campus library services as part of the job description.   _____

7. SUPPORT STAFF:

At least one member of the support staff has either full-time or part-time responsibilities for off-campus library services as part of the job description.   _____

8. BIBLIOGRAPHIC INSTRUCTION:

A librarian provides direct bibliographic instruction to off-campus students by visits to course sites, through teleconferencing, or by use of audio-visual media such as videotape.   _____

9. ONLINE BIBLIOGRAPHIC SERVICES:

Online literature searches are conducted for off-campus students on request.   _____

10. INTERLIBRARY LOANS:

I.L.L. requests for material not available from the "home" library are initiated by library staff on behalf of off-campus students.   _____

11. CHARGES FOR SERVICE:

All library services for off-campus students are provided free-of-charge.   _____

12. NEEDS ASSESSMENTS:

The library staff undertakes formal or informal needs assessments for off-campus courses and programs and uses this information to plan library services.   _____

13. EVALUATION:

   The library staff periodically reviews the
services and resources available to off-campus
students and evaluates their effectiveness.   _____

ADDITIONAL COMMENTS:

_____

_____

_____

_____

_____

_____

Appendix C

Report of Survey Results by Library: Single Value Description of Categories

Library Name	Core Col.	Sp.Req.	Ref.Q.	Phone	Advert.	Libr'n	Support	Bib.Instr	Online	ILL	Charge	Assess	Eval	Totals
Acadia Univ.	1	1	1	0	0	0	0	0	1	1	0	0	0	5
Athabasca Univ.	0	1	1	0	1	1	1	0	1	1	1	0	0	8
Brandon Univ.	1	1	1	1	1	1	1	1	1	1	1	1	1	13
Brock Univ.	1	0	0	0	1	0	1	1	1	1	1	1	1	9
Lakehead Univ.	1	1	1	1	1	1	1	0	1	0	1	1	1	11
Laurentian Univ.	1	1	1	1	1	0	1	0	0	1	1	1	0	9
Memorial Univ.	0	1	1	0	0	0	0	0	0	0	0	0	0	2
Mount St. Vincent Univ.	1	1	1	0	1	0	1	0	1	0	1	1	1	9
Open Learning Inst.	0	1	1	1	1	1	0	1	0	1	1	1	1	10
Queen's Univ.	0	1	0	0	1	0	0	0	0	0	0	0	0	2
Simon Fraser Univ.	0	1	1	1	1	1	1	0	1	1	1	1	1	11

Appendix C (continued)

Library Name	Core Col.	Sp.Req.	Ref.Q.	Phone	Advert.	Libr'n	Support	Bib.Instr	Online	ILL	Charge	Assess	Eval	Totals
Trent Univ.	1	1	1	1	1	0	1	1	1	1	1	1	1	12
U. of Alberta	1	1	1	0	0	0	0	1	1	0	0	1	1	7
U. of British Columbia	1	1	1	1	1	1	1	0	1	1	1	1	1	12
U. of Calgary	1	1	1	0	0	0	0	1	1	1	0	1	1	8
U. of Lethbridge	1	1	0	0	0	0	0	0	1	0	1	0	1	5
U. of Manitoba	1	1	1	0	1	1	1	1	1	1	1	1	1	12
U. of Ottawa	1	1	1	0	1	1	0	1	1	1	1	1	1	11
U. of P.E.I.	1	0	0	0	0	0	0	0	0	0	1	0	0	2
U. of Saskatchewan	1	1	1	0	1	0	0	0	0	0	1	0	0	5
U. of Victoria	1	1	1	1	1	1	1	1	1	1	1	1	1	13
U. of W. Ontario	1	1	1	1	1	1	1	0	0	0	0	0	1	8
U. of Windsor	1	0	0	0	0	0	1	0	0	0	1	0	1	4
York Univ.	0	1	1	0	0	0	1	1	0	0	0	1	1	6
Totals	18	21	19	9	16	10	14	10	15	13	17	15	17	194

Report of Survey Results by Library: Multiple Value Description of Categories

Library Name	Core Col.	Sp.Req.	Ref.Q.	Phone	Advert.	Libr'n	Support	Bib.Instr	Online	ILL	Charge	Assess	Eval	Totals
Acadia Univ.	1	1	1	0	0	0	0	0	2	2	0	0	0	7
Athabasca Univ.	0	1	1	0	2	2	2	0	2	2	2	0	0	14
Brandon Univ.	1	1	1	2	2	2	2	2	2	2	2	3	3	25
Brock Univ.	1	0	0	0	2	0	2	2	2	2	2	3	3	19
Lakehead Univ.	1	1	1	2	2	2	2	0	2	0	2	3	3	21
Laurentian Univ.	1	1	1	2	2	0	2	0	0	2	2	3	0	16
Memorial Univ.	0	1	1	0	0	0	0	0	0	0	0	0	0	2
Mount St. Vincent Univ.	1	1	1	0	2	0	2	0	2	0	2	3	3	17
Open Learning Inst.	0	1	1	2	2	2	0	2	0	2	2	3	3	20
Queen's Univ.	0	1	0	0	2	0	0	0	0	0	0	0	0	3
Simon Fraser Univ.	0	1	1	2	2	2	2	0	2	2	2	3	3	22

Appendix D (continued)

Library Name	Core Col.	Sp.Req.	Ref.Q.	Phone	Advert.	Libr'n	Support	Bib.Instr	Online	ILL	Charge	Assess	Eval	Totals
Trent Univ.	1	1	1	2	2	0	2	2	2	2	2	3	3	23
U. of Alberta	1	1	1	0	0	0	0	2	2	0	0	3	3	13
U. of British Columbia	1	1	1	2	2	2	2	0	2	2	2	3	3	23
U. of Calgary	1	1	1	0	0	0	0	2	2	2	0	3	3	15
U. of Lethbridge	1	1	0	0	0	0	0	0	2	0	2	0	3	9
U. of Manitoba	1	1	1	0	2	2	2	2	2	2	2	3	3	23
U. of Ottawa	1	1	1	0	2	2	0	2	2	2	2	3	3	21
U. of P.E.I.	1	0	0	0	0	0	0	0	0	0	2	0	0	3
U. of Saskatchewan	1	1	1	0	2	0	0	0	0	0	2	0	0	7
U. of Victoria	1	1	1	2	2	2	2	2	2	2	2	3	3	25
U. of W. Ontario	1	1	1	2	2	2	2	0	0	0	0	0	3	14
U. of Windsor	1	0	0	0	0	0	2	0	0	0	2	0	3	8
York Univ.	0	1	1	0	0	0	2	2	0	0	0	3	3	12

Appendix E

Report of Survey Results By Library: Hierarchical Comparison
of Appendices C & D

Library Name	Total Appendix C	Total Appendix D
Brandon University	13	25
University of Victoria	13	25
Trent University	12	23
University of British Columbia	12	23
University of Manitoba	12	23
Simon Fraser University	11	22
Lakehead University	11	21
University of Ottawa	11	21
Open Learning Institute	10	20
Brock University	9	19
Mount St. Vincent University	9	17
Laurentian University	9	16
University of Calgary	8	15
Athabasca University	8	14
University of Western Ontario	8	14
University of Alberta	7	13
York University	6	12
University of Lethbridge	5	9
University of Windsor	4	8
Acadia University	5	7
University of Saskatchewan	5	7
Queen's University	2	3
University of Prince Edward Island	2	3
Memorial University	2	2

Library Development as a Catalyst
for Continuing Education Innovation
in a Major Research University:
A Case Study[1]

Mary Joyce Pickett and Brian Nielsen

With an Addendum Co-authored by

Susan Swords Steffen

The role of continuing education programming at a branch campus of a major private research university differs significantly from such programming in a state-supported or private service-oriented institution. Without a clearly articulated institutional focus on service to the surrounding community, a branch campus program may suffer from scant management attention, despite the clear demographic trend toward a growing adult learner, and shrinking the adult resident student population. This paper will describe the efforts of library staff working in conjunction with continuing education managers to enhance continuing education programming through library development. Using the managerial perspective provided by Rosabeth Kanter (1982), the strategy for change may best be understood as the exercise of middle-management entrepreneurship "from below," rather than a top-down push for innovation in continuing education.

Northwestern University's Division of Continuing Education operates primarily on the institution's downtown Chicago campus, ten miles from its main campus in suburban Evanston. The Schaffner Library, a branch of the University Library, has had a mission to serve the Continuing Education Division, as well as the extension Master's in Management program of the Graduate School of Management, though services and collection at that branch were essentially static from 1972 to 1981. The case of recent developments in Schaffner Library is here described as a case to illustrate the strategy for institutional change that moves from the library to the larger continuing education program.

Kanter's study of 165 middle managers in five companies describes characteristics of successful middle management which she argues to be critical for the United States' return to a position of economic leadership in the world. Kanter, a professor of sociology and management at Yale University, shows middle managers, not always top executives, leading the way to corporate innovation and increased productivity through "working smart;" in like fashion, we hope to show that academic library middle managers can effect major changes in service delivery to extended campus students and faculty. Borrowing from Kanter's conclusions about what makes for high effectiveness in corporate middle management, we offer through a description of service development in a library serving adult learners some suggestions about what may lead to success in library innovation. In a nutshell, Kanter enumerates five qualities in middle managers which may lead to high innovativeness. These are: 1) comfort with change; 2) clarity of direction; 3) thoroughness; 4) participative management style; and 5) persuasiveness, persistence, and discretion.

The library we will described today is the Joseph Schaffner Library, a branch library of Northwestern University Library, serving students in Northwestern's University College and in the Graduate School of Management's night school MBA program, called the "Manager's Program." The University College is Northwestern's administrative unit for adult continuing education certificate and degree programs, and both the University College and the Manager's Program are located on Northwestern's downtown Chicago campus, two blocks from the Second City's fashionable Million Dollar Mile, but ten miles from the main campus in Evanston, Illinois. Schaffner Library, the University College, and the Manager's Program all occupy the same building.

The recent history of Schaffner Library is a story of exodus, decline, and recent renaissance. The critical event for the Schaffner Library in the last decade was the university's decision to move the management school from Chicago to the Evanston campus, an important step for the university in developing that school into one of the prominent graduate management programs in the United States. When the school moved, so did most of the book collection and staff in the Schaffner Library, leaving behind in the facility a small paraprofessional staff, about 70,000 volumes, perhaps 150 active journal subscriptions, all for the use of students in night classes which remained on the Chicago campus. No librarians were left to do book selection or provide reference services; the only material funds remaining there were for the purchase of books for reserve. The situation remained essentially stagnant for nearly a decade, until aid to the facility was identified in 1979 as a possible addendum to a major University Library National Endowment for the Humanities Challenge Grant fund-raising program. Surprising to the University Library, the Schaffner component of the campaign was immediately successful, and the Library was faced with spending several thousand dollars without much notion of what materials were needed by the patrons of Schaffner Library. Though bibliographers on the Evanston campus did purchase several hundred monographs, they were selecting "in the dark," so to speak, and recommended that a special assessment be undertaken of the need for service delivery in Schaffner. With NEH funding, it was decided to create a one-year professional position to explore service development in the downtown facility, the position to be called the Schaffner Project Librarian.

This paper's first author was hired as the Schaffner Project Librarian in September of 1983; the second author was at the time a member of the search committee for the positions, as well as being head of the main library reference department. Working together, and with many other staff both within and outside the library system at Northwestern, the project librarian and the head of reference began to redefine the service priorities of Schaffner, accomplishing considerable innovation within the space of a year.

One of the project librarian's first activities was to gather information about Schaffner Library, other University Libraries, and University College. Information about Northwestern University Libraries was obtained through interviews with personnel representing over twenty areas of responsibility. As the project developed, we found that working with people from reference, circulation, cataloging, reserves, collection management, interlibrary loan, and other Chicago campus libraries was important.

Observation at the Schaffner Library, including some evening and Saturday hours, provided a preliminary understanding of clientele and usage there. A meeting with continuing education English faculty, instructional sessions in classes, and follow-up reference appointments by approximately ten students provided first hand information about University College faculty and students. This preliminary gathering of information resulted in the following observations:

1. Although some students had developed basic library skills, other had literally no knowledge of library tools and research processes(e.g.,

two students who scheduled reference interviews had never heard of the *Readers' Guide* until the presentation to their class).

2. Even though most of the students are juggling their coursework around full-time jobs, their commitment is considerable. The students who signed up for reference appointments were there are the appointed time and very appreciative.

3. Northwestern continuing education students need to be made more fully aware of resources available through Northwestern University Libraries. However, because of their diverse backgrounds and situations, bibliographic instruction should be centered around the research process and not restricted to use of a specific library. Karen Brown discussed the importance of teaching transferable research strategies to adult part-time learners in a paper at the 1982 Off-campus Library Services Conference (Brown, 1982).

4. Although the Schaffner Library was tied into the University Library's on-line public access catalog, there was no educational program explaining the system.

5. Once a University College student using the on-line catalog identified a title needed in the main University Library, he or she had to make a trip to Evanston for it; there was no document delivery system between Evanston and Chicago campus libraries. Even worse, University College students had to follow special procedures to obtain a borrowing card for the Evanston campus libraries. Students going there evenings or weekends who had not gotten a card in advance could not check out books. Needless to say this created considerable ill will.

6. The reference collection was inadequate and difficult to use, having numerous shelving sequences. Two classification systems were in use, with the older materials, ironically, in LC, and the newer in Dewey.

7. During the peak one or two hours immediately preceding classes the library was very crowded. At other times it was almost empty.

These observations revealed glaring deficiencies in the library services provided to Northwestern's part-time adult learners. In November 1983 University College administrators were invited to join University Library administrators and the project librarian in a meeting to begin redefinition of library services for University College students. This redefinition included these recommendations:

1. Improved access (for University College students) to the main University Library. University College students were the only group of Northwestern University students not automatically issued ID cards which could be used to charge out library materials. The automatic issuance of ID cards to University College students was strongly recommended. In addition, programs to acquaint these students with the facilities of the main University Library needed to be developed.

2. Improved document delivery service between campuses. Monographic items should be received in one day and photocopies in two.

3. Reorganization and expansion of the reference collection at Schaffner. This would involve identifying older LC classed reference titles to remain in the collection and be reclassified into Dewey, selection of additional titles, and rearrangement of the collection into one shelving sequence.

4. The institution of on-line searching as an additional reference tool at Schaffner. In cases where it was to be used in lieu of purchasing the print index, the searches should be subsidized.

5. Provision of qualified reference and bibliographic instruction personnel. The project librarian's experience demonstrated a need for instruction in the research process and the use of reference tools. A reference librarian should be available during late afternoon and early evening hours when most students are on campus.

6. Additional study space. In addition to these proposals for immediate service improvement, a more general proposal was made which was to have important implications for Schaffner's future. The head of reference proposed Schaffner be designated a special "library laboratory" for information delivery experiments. The "library laboratory" idea suggested the possibility that Schaffner could take advantage of Northwestern's advance ground for smaller experiments, such as with end user on-line searching, electronic delivery of full texts, and use of the university's fiber optic link between the Evanston and Chicago campuses for message transmission between the libraries. This suggestion, in line with Kanter's notion of providing overall clarity

of direction for innovation, was immediately attractive to the University College administrators, and proved helpful in garnering additional support for the larger innovation proposed.

The project librarian prepared a proposed 1984-85 Schaffner Library budget which would enable beginning development of the above services. A document outlining the rationale and potential of the library laboratory concept at Schaffner was prepared by the head of reference. This accompanied the budget document which included a request for personnel to investigate research possibilities. The budget was completed and approved by the University College and University Library administrations in February 1984. The support of University College administrators was crucial for obtaining University approval, which was received in early August 1984.

By the spring of 1984 there was movement for actual program implementation, combining resources from both the library and the parent university. Reference titles most appropriate for the collection were identified and ordering begun. Arrangements were made with the cataloging department of the University Library to have those reference titles still in LC reclassified to Dewey and entered into the on-line catalog.

An early political move to alert the faculty to the project was a letter sent to all Spring Semester 1984 University College faculty explaining the project, outlining recommendations made to date, and requesting that they inform the project librarian of their library-related concerns. Seventeen faculty responded with a range of concerns including titles recommendations, problems with the reserve system, problems with locating materials in the Schaffner Library, and requests for instructional sessions in their classes. Six sessions (three on the Chicago campus and three in Evanston) were arranged as a result of the letter. Several faculty made general comments supportive of steps to improve services. Feedback from the instructional sessions was positive and notes about the sessions describing strengths and weaknesses were kept on file to refer to if future programs were to develop.

Considerable ill will resulted from the special procedures required of University College students to obtain a library card. The first step of public relations campaign directed to students was a letter explaining the process, recognizing the inconvenience caused, and indicating that procedures for automatic issuance of cards were being developed. Approximately fifty percent more students requested cards in the Spring 1984 semester than in the Spring 1983 semester.

A brief guide to the Schaffner Library was completed and available for patrons. It was distributed in Chicago campus instructional sessions along with guides to the main University Library and a brochure describing the use of the on-line catalog (LUIS).

Delivery between the two campuses was unsatisfactory utilizing the regular campus mail system. In February the University Library instituted an arrangement with the University Purchasing and Stores delivery truck to deliver library materials between the two campuses. This proved to be more dependable but still did not provide direct library-to-library delivery.

Additional study space was created by moving excess shelving (left by the withdrawal of dead periodical runs), painting, and adding study tables.

Throughout the project questions arose regarding current use of the Schaffner Library. Patron counts were available for some time periods. Additional counts were instituted. To ascertain who used the library and for what purposes, a patron survey was conducted the weeks of March 5 and May 7, 1985. A stratified sample of two hour time blocks was drawn for weekday surveying. Surveying was done the entire day on Saturdays. Over 80% of entering library users took survey forms. Valid forms were returned by 89% or 351 users. Of the patrons surveyed 45% were affiliated with the Manager's Program, 33% with University College, 19% with other Northwestern schools (9% with Medical 6% Law, and 4% other), and 3% were non-Northwestern people.

Saturday users were predominately Manager's Program students (67% of users on March 10 and 56% on May 14 with University College students accounting for only 12% of users each Saturday). More extensive use of reserve materials and computer rooms adjacent to the library partially accounts for the heavier use by Manager's Program students. In addition to being the largest user group, the Manager's students were the most vocal in the comments' section of the questionnaire.

Patrons were asked to indicate library services they used during their visit. Study space was as expected the most frequently checked response. Most responses were consistent with casual observation and with what limited statistics were already available. For instance, the use of reserves reported was consistent with reserve circulation statistics. While 16% of University College respondents used the card catalog and 11% the online catalog, only 7% of Manager's Program respondents used the card catalog and 6% used the on-line catalog. In contrast, the percentages of each group actually using reference books (Manager's Program--13%; University College--11%) and circulating books (Manager's Program--12%; University College--13%) was very similar. What this means is that management students often use familiar reference tools (*Value Line, Moody's,* etc.) and do not need to refer to the catalog. In looking for circulating books they also may be more apt to go directly to the shelves since the scope of subjects they use is more limited. It may also mean that when they do use the catalog, management students are more apt to find the books they need at Schaffner than are University College students. As was expected, very few respondents (4%) reported asking for reference assistance. Follow-up surveys can help determine if use of this and other services increases when regularly scheduled reference service and bibliographic instruction programs are instituted.

Because the project librarian had been hired with NEH funds raised primarily by the Division of Continuing Education, she had been directed to examine the library needs of students in that division. Throughout the project it had become increasingly clear that planning for the Schaffner Library should also consider the needs of Manager's Program students. The survey confirmed this assumption, and the project librarian strongly recommended formal involvement of Manager's Program faculty and administration in future planning. The formation of an Extended Campus Services Library Advisory committee was recommended. This committee would include representatives of both programs.

With budget adoption, the Schaffner Library was placed administratively under the reference department of the University Library. The search for an extended campus services librarian to implement and coordinate improved library services to nontraditional students on both the main and the satellite campus was begun. University College and Manager's Program administrators participated in the search process. A librarian was appointed to begin in February

1985 as a member of the Northwestern University Library Reference Department and Head of the Schaffner Library.

The creation of a research office in the University Library occurred shortly before approval of the Schaffner budget. Once the Schaffner budget was funded to provide improved traditional library services for nontraditional students, the library laboratory concept at Schaffner became a logical choice for early projects of this office. The Schaffner budget included funding for an eighteen month half-time person to investigate possible projects and prepare proposals for funding. Alternatives being investigated particularly applicable to a remote site serving busy nontraditional students (mostly employed full-time and taking evening courses) include:

1. Creating model curriculum modules for teaching adult learners aspects of information management. We have been in contact with University College faculty teaching writing and public policy studies to consider offering endorser training, database creation and management, and the use of computer communications programs as components of regular coursework in the college. A proposal for a federal grant to implement this aspect of the Schaffner plan has been developed.

2. Developing enhancements to the Northwestern online integrated system to provide more useful services to adult continuing education students. We would like to see Schaffner patrons be able to search the on-line catalog strictly for materials in that branch library, rather than only in the union catalog mode; similarly, we would like to see Schaffner users be able to request well-formatted printouts of bibliographic citations found in the catalog, rather than using a simple screen printer.

3. Providing documents for use in the Schaffner Library through electronic means. Because we can experimentally isolate some extent, we may try providing students with access to such services as Information Access Corporation's "ASAP," or documents available experimentally on videodisc.

Several conclusions which can be drawn from Northwestern's experience are relevant for other institutions planning library services for nontraditional students. First, an effective program requires library-wide cooperation. Kanter's call for a participative management style and for thoroughness dovetail nicely with this conclusion. Planning involved consultation with personnel in many departments including reference, collection management, interlibrary loan, circulation, cataloging, acquisition, and other Chicago campus libraries. This same cooperation is crucial as implementation is taking place. Needless to say, support of the library administration is critical at all stages of planning and implementation.

Second, the support of appropriate academic administrators is crucial. Here, Kanter's notions of persuasiveness and discretion come into play. The academic administrators served as valuable political allies for library middle managers in their efforts to convince upper management within the library of the need to move forward to implement needed change. They can provide valuable information about curriculum, faculty, and students for library planners. At Northwestern we found that academic traditional services and new technology in serving busy nontraditional students. A major factor in approval of the 1984-85 Schaffner budget was the support of University College administration in approaching the University for funding.

Third, patience and flexibility are required. As Kanter notes that change is often difficult to effect in large organizations, we had to know when to move slowly, when to contact other staff, when to bring in additional minds for decision making. Some things did not go as planned. Although we had verbal approval on the creation of a new Extended Campus Services Librarian position in the spring of 1984, formal approval of the budget for it did not come until late in the summer, forcing an interruption in service provision by a graduate librarian for several months in Schaffner between the time of the departure of the Schaffner Project Librarian and the arrival of the incumbent in the new position. Our planning had to allow for that kind of flexibility.

Finally, effective promotion is essential in creating a successful program. It was very apparent throughout the project that outreach and communication would need to be given top priority in the implementation of services. Many nontraditional students and the faculty who teach them were unaware of the library services which were already available to them. There is little purpose in creating new and expanded services if they are not publicized. Plans for the Schaffner project stressed outreach to students and faculty.

Addendum

Susan Swords Steffen and Brian Nielsen

During the past five years, the Schaffner Library has been transformed
from a remote outpost with a tentative future to a busy, successful
center for library services. Each year an extensive user education
program provides instruction to over 1,000 students. In 1989-90, over
2,000 items were delivered from the main campus. Active use is made
of nine CD-ROM products, several online search services, and
Northwestern's LUIS and other local online catalogs. A professional
and paraprofessional staff of seven coordinates and delivers a variety
of well-used library services to students on the University's Chicago
campus. The Library has been reorganized and rejuvenated to meet
these service demands, and the University Library has committed
additional resources to the project. Schaffner has recently received a
major grant from the W.K. Kellogg Foundation to begin renovation of
its facilities and to expand and evaluate its programs. Recognition of
the value of Schaffner's program has been heightened by numerous
publications on the library's innovations,[2] and internally within the
University through the recognition that the Kellogg Foundation grant
has brought.

Over the same period, University College (the current name of the
Division of Continuing Education) has flourished, the library playing
a significant role in its success. Its enrollment decline has not only
been halted but reversed, and now over 2,000 students participate in
the program. The College has undertaken many initiatives to improve
and insure the quality of its programs. In support of a new writing
requirement for matriculating students, the Library has become home
to the Chicago Writing Place, a tutoring service which provides
assistance to students with writing problems. A faculty development
program designed to increase the skills and commitment of extension
faculty features regular participation from the Library at training
sessions for new faculty, faculty seminars, and departmental and
faculty-wide programs. To address the broader needs of adults in their
returning student roles, Schaffner's user education programs have
focused on the problems of confidence, basic skills improvement, and
time management as well as information literacy skills.

The application of information technology and technological change have been central themes throughout Schaffner's development. Although the projects proposed in the original "electronic library laboratory" concept have not been implemented, the library has followed where technology has led. During the past five years, CD-ROM has emerged as a practical and affordable technology which provides powerful research opportunities to an extension campus. At Schaffner, CD-ROM tools have virtually replaced print indexes for access to journal articles. Our initial attempts to use a microcomputer for transfer of intercampus loan requests have been superseded by the introduction of the telefacsimile machine. Participation in the online circulation subsystem of NOTIS and the provision of local printing for LUIS have improved the delivery and handling of intercampus loan requests.

Allocation of staff resources, availability of information technology, and interdepartmental cooperation have been critical factors in the success of this project. But, as noted five years ago in our earliest writing on Schaffner, a participative management style, building support from senior academic administrators, flexibility in deployment of long-term plans, and continuing promotion of service all also contribute to a vital program for adult continuing promotion of service all also contribute to a vital program for adult continuing education students.

Among the most remarkable changes brought about by the transformation of the Schaffner Library has been the fresh attitude toward experimental service development on the part of senior library administrators. The Schaffner initiative involved taking a risk: there was no urgent expression of "need" from adult continuing education students for library services, but a sense of the value of service enhancement on the part of a few librarians who were aware of the changing nature of technology and of student demographics. It will be important for other libraries to experiment with new models for serving adult students, as in the future this group will become even more important to our universities.

References

Brown, K. (1982). A bibliographic instruction model for reaching adult part-time students. In B.M. Lessin (Ed.), *The Off-campus Library Services Conference Proceedings: St. Louis, Missouri, October 14-15, 1982*, (pp. 169-73). Mount Pleasant, MI: Central Michigan University Press.

Kanter, R. (1982). The middle manager as innovator. *Harvard Business Review*, *60*(4), 95-105.

Notes

[1] The paper prepared by Mary Joyce Pickett and Brian Nielsen was presented at the second Off-campus Library Services Conference, Knoxville, Tennessee and appeared in the 1986 edition of the conference proceedings.

[2] Other publications on Schaffner Library include: Jean Alexander and Susan Swords Steffen, "Library Services for Part-Time Management Students: What They Want and What They Need," In Barton Lessin, ed., *The Off-campus Library Services Conference Proceedings* [Mount Pleasant, MI, Central Michigan University Press, 1989] pp. 1-12; Betsy Baker and Susan Swords Steffen, "Microcomputers and Bibliographic Instruction," *Reference Librarian* 24: 223-32, (1989); Susan Swords Steffen, "College Faculty Goes Online: Training Faculty to Search," *Journal of Academic Librarianship* 12 (3): 147-151, (July 1986); Susan Swords Steffen, "Designing Bibliographic Instruction Programs for Adult Students: The Schaffner Library Experience," *Illinois Libraries* 70: 644-9, (December 1988); Susan Swords Steffen, "Faculty As End Users: Strategies, Challenges, and Rewards," *Bibliographic Instruction and Computer Database Searching: Papers Presented at the Fourteenth National LOEX Library Instruction Conference* [Ann Arbor, Michigan: Pierian Press, 1989]; Susan Swords Steffen and Hilary Ward, "The Library As An Agent of Quality In An Off-Campus Program," *National Issues In Higher Education*, No. 23 [Kansas State University, 1986]; Susan Swords Steffen, "Living With and Managing Change: A Case Study of the Schaffner Library," *Illinois Libraries* 69: 126-9, (February 1987); Susan Swords Steffen, "Partnership for Quality: Non-Traditional Students and the Librarian," In *The Librarian in the University: Essays on Membership in the Academic Community*, Palmer Hall and Caroline Byrd, eds. [Metuchen, NJ: Scarecrow Press, 1990]; Susan Swords Steffen, "A Reference Librarian's Point of View (of tampering with the online catalog)," *Journal of Academic Librarianship* 12: 341-3, (January 1987); Susan Swords Steffen, "Working with Part-time Faculty: Challenges and Rewards," In Barton Lessin, ed., *The Off-campus Library Services*

Conference Proceedings [Mount Pleasant, MI, Central Michigan University Press, 1987] pp. 306-314; Hillary Ward and Susan Swords Steffen, "Building Confident Scholars: The Library As Agent of Excellence in Adult Education," *Proceedings of the Sixth National Conference on Adult and External Degree Programs*, October 1986, 147-156.

Developing Branch Campus Libraries:
The Administrative Perspective[1]

Barbara E. Kemp and Maureen Pastine

As a land grant institution, Washington State University (WSU) has as part of its mission service to the citizens of the state. While service has been broadly interpreted and includes many activities, provision of academic courses and programs in a variety of formats and locations has long been a tradition. Access to academic offerings throughout a primarily rural state is seen as a strong component of the service mission and has helped to maintain a continuing, positive presence for WSU. This is especially important in light of the university's isolated location in the extreme southeastern area of the state. The academic offerings range from correspondence courses to single (often short) courses in response to specific community interests to full degree or certificate programs.

The offering of degree programs off-campus has tapped the growing population of working adults who want the opportunity to further their education but to not have the luxury of being full-time resident students on any campus. Many drive long distances to attend the class sessions. The demand for such programs has increased thought the 1980's and, not surprisingly, has been generated in three large population centers not otherwise served by a research university. Vancouver, located in extreme southwestern Washington, on the border with Oregon; Spokane, located in northeastern Washington, near but not within commuting distance of WSU; and the cities of Richland, Pasco, and Kennewick (collectively known as the Tri-Cities), in south-central Washington, at the hub of the nuclear energy industry. Each of these areas were developed as a center for off-campus educational access, with each having different program needs and on-site facilities. These differences were, if anything, magnified in the needs for library services, resources, and facilities.

When degree programs were first developed, there was relatively little consultation with or involvement by the WSU Libraries. Library services at the off-campus centers grew on an almost ad hoc basis. In Vancouver, WSU contracted with Cannell Library of Clark College, a local community college to house materials, provide a .5 FTE professional position, and some reference and reserve services. The original engineering program in Vancouver was supported by legislative funding for a "technical library" and some continuing funding for personnel and acquisitions. WSU Libraries' faculty consulted on the original development of the technical library, but continuing operations were the responsibility of Cannell Library personnel. Although purchased on WSU funds, technical library materials were acquired and cataloged by Cannell Library and did not appear in the WSU Libraries' catalogs. In the future, new acquisitions will be acquired, cataloged and processed at WSU Libraries in Pullman prior to shipment to Cannell Library for location and access.

In contrast to Vancouver, Spokane is served by higher education institutions beyond the community college level. Engineering and computer science courses and programs have been developed in cooperation with Gonzaga University, and WSU students in these programs have access to the Gonzaga University Library. Similarly, a cooperative nursing program has a separately staffed and funded center, known as the Intercollegiate Center for Nursing Education (ICNE). This center has a separately staffed and funded library facility, but the WSU Libraries purchase and catalog some materials which are housed in the ICNE Library. Such items do appear in the WSU Libraries' catalogs.

Five state universities cooperate in the Tri-Cities University Center (TUC). Not administered by WSU, the TUC has a separately funded and staffed library, which has outgrown its physical facility. Materials have not been purchased either directly or indirectly by the WSU Libraries, but WSU holdings have been available to TUC students through interlibrary loan.

In 1984, the introduction of a master's degree program in education at the Vancouver center highlighted the problems with this laissez-faire provision of library support. The program was initiated without consulting the WSU Libraries, with chaotic results. Everyone involved discovered very rapidly that the education courses relied much more heavily on library resources than did engineering and computer science courses. It was also very apparent that the local community college and public libraries did not have collections to support graduate work in education. The WSU Libraries were immediately called upon to solve the problem, which we did, but unfortunately we had no real policies or procedures, let alone a plan, to provide library support to our off-campus centers. A partnership between the WSU Libraries and Continuing Education and Public Service (CEPS), the university unit responsible for developing and monitoring off-campus programs, developed. Under aggressive leadership and with the help of many individuals contacted at earlier Off-Campus Library Services conferences, chaos became order. By the end of 1985, a plan for flexible delivery of materials and services had been developed. Under this plan, materials would be provided through a combination of on-site and "travelling" collections, with the on-site emphasis being on the provision of finding tools. Access to the WSU Libraries in Pullman was provided by dial-up access to the on-line catalog, site location of the union list of serials microfiche, and an 800 telephone number. Materials would be mailed directly to the user, avoiding traditional interlibrary loan. Underlying this plan was the rationale that a major research library could not be duplicated even once, let alone at multiple sites, so the central campus collections had to be available to all. Special or unusual services were needed to compensate for the otherwise unequal access to the collections. The plan was implemented in 1986 with no extra staff. It proved so popular that in 1987 the WSU Libraries received funding for 1.5 FTE to be devoted exclusively to administering and providing library support to our off-campus students and staff and to expanding and refining the program.

Also in 1987, at the same time the WSU Libraries were receiving additional staff to provide library support, the state legislature gave WSU the mandate to develop the Vancouver and Spokane centers into a formal multi-campus system. The TUC was included too, but implementation of the administrative change was scheduled for a year later, in 1988. This move to multi-campus status has brought about some significant changes. The simple fact of an improved, formal status lends even more weight to the programs offered. Upper division undergraduate programs are being offered in Vancouver and resident instructional faculty are now being transferred or hired to work at the multi-campus sites. This latter development has created a significant difference in terms of library support. Previously the concern was provision of library services to support the curriculum. Now the WSU Libraries must also support the research and tenure/promotion needs of faculty researchers in a multi-campus system. Even the names have been changed. CEPS has become Extended Academic Programs (EAP) within the division of Extended University Services. We no longer talk of "off-campus" programs either. Full partnership with the Pullman campus is now indicated by "multi-campus." Perhaps the most significant change, however, has been the consolidation of responsibility for the development and provision of library support for a multi-campus system under the aegis of the Director of WSU Libraries. Formerly this responsibility was shared by the WSU Libraries, CEPS/EAP and local site libraries. Having formal administrative responsibility has allowed the WSU Libraries the authority to begin and shape short and long-range planning, especially for the budget process. The original (1985) plan continues to be examined to see which elements can be retained, which should be altered, and which, if any, need to be eliminated.

As noted earlier, all three of the developing campuses have some form of on-site library facility, yet they are all in different stages of development. A centralized facility for WSU-Spokane has been developed and includes space for a small library/reading room. The intent is to bring most of the program offerings to this central facility (the nursing program being the exception) and to consolidate library support in the same location. While this is certainly an appropriate move, the library is hampered by the lack of any on-site staff to maintain and protect the collections. Pressures are developing to establish "full service" libraries in each location rather than maintaining staffed reading rooms. Realistically, it must be remembered that is not financially possible to duplicate a full research library in three separate locations. Politically, such a demand would be legislative suicide. However, the growing concerns of the developing campus administrators and faculty on this topic must be addressed. The basic questions in this area are: a) how fast should the new campus libraries grow; and b) how large should they become?

Staffing problems are a major administrative concern, which also overlap into local site and campus political concerns. Gaining control of staffing means greater uniformity in the provision of services and greater control in establishing and applying policies and procedures. Provisions must be made to keep library faculty and staff on all campuses in close contact and to prevent isolation or overly independent action, divergent from a "system" concept. The transfer from contracted services to WSU site personnel also is a delicate matter, since loss of outside funding is always a blow to any budget.

This local concern must also be viewed in the context of inter-institutional politics. Although none of the developing campuses exist near research library facilities, all are located where there are local public and college libraries. It is reasonable to expect that some demand for library support will continue to be made on these libraries, regardless of the services provided by the WSU Libraries. Such demands obviously do not justify formal contracted services, but such local concerns must be acknowledged and addressed.

Campus politics also enter into the picture. Not everyone on the Pullman campus is wholeheartedly behind the multi-campus development, and one of the first areas of concern that is mentioned is that of library support. Critics charge that it is obvious that adequate library support cannot be provided at a distance, especially without draining already strained resources from the Pullman campus.

WSU has begun to address some of these concerns on a campus-wide basis. In the fall of 1987, all major campus administrators devoted one day of a two-day leadership conference to discussion of concerns relating to developing a multi-campus system. Of course, library support was only one of the many issues raised, but having a forum in which to openly raise and discuss concerns did much to allay unnecessary fears. This same method was latter extended in a series of meetings for all faculty on the Pullman campus.

These initial forums led to the establishment of a number of task forces on the WSU campus. One of the appointed task forces was on library services at developing campuses. This task force was made up of the Director of Libraries, the head of Science Libraries, the head of Humanities/Social Sciences Public Services, the Director of Instructional Media Services, the head of Off-Campus Library Services, the WSU Libraries' Systems Librarian, the head of the ICNE Library, the head of the Tri-Cities University Center Library, a representative of EAPS, two teaching faculty members, and an off-campus research faculty member.

The Task Force on Library Services at Developing Campuses completed a comprehensive planning document, with the following major recommendations:

1. All developing branch campuses will rely on the main (WSU-Pullman) campus libraries for major library research resources and services.

2. The WSU-Pullman Director of Libraries and Executive Directors

of the three off-campus centers will share final authority and decision-making responsibilities in regard to libraries and library personnel, but the Director of Libraries will be given signature authority for funds expenditure.

3. Small reading room library facilities will be provided at the WSU-Spokane and WSU-Vancouver sites and library space will be expanded in the Tri-Cities center, as there are fewer strong local library collections in the Tri-Cities. In addition, a potential merger of the Battelle Library (in Richland) and the Tri-Cities University Center Library will be explored.

4. Cooperative library agreements and contractual library services with appropriate area libraries to assist in provision of reference and clerical support, library resources, etc., will be formalized (e.g., written and signed agreements) to reduce problems and resentments arising from the informal agreements of previous years.

5. All on-site library facilities (and some of those area libraries with extensive contractual services) will be equipped with a toll-free telephone access to WSU-Pullman, search-only capabilities to the Western Library Network (the WSU Libraries' catalog), electronic mail capabilities, a telefacsimile machine, a photocopy machine, a microcomputer terminal to be used for related word processing and record keeping capabilities, and microforms reader/printer, and adequate seating and shelving if these are not already available on-site.

6. Each on-site reading room library facility will be equipped with adequate professional and clerical staff to cover needed hours of service and to provide limited public service assistance.

7. Adequate funding for periodic travel to and from sites will be provided to library personnel at all sites.

The Task Force Report on Library Services at Developing Campuses also identified and analyzed successful models for provision of library services to extended campus programs and then proposed an appropriate system for organization and delivery of library resources to be implemented by WSU. The final plan relied extensively on electronic transmission of requests for service and data delivery, but it also included the development of small reserve, reference, monographic and serial collections at each branch-campus site along with limited staffing to serve each site. The overall policy is that branch campus students and faculty are entitled to the same basic services as provided on the Pullman campus: efficient access to materials required for their courses; access to a wide range of monographs and periodicals needed for course research; basic and advanced reference assistance; access to specialized library services such as library user education presentations, computer literature searching, and interlibrary loan. The challenge in making such services available necessitates funding for provision of varied, innovative, and flexible services and variations in policies and procedures to accommodate differing access and assistance methodologies. A well-developed budget request was included in the report. The use of WHETS (Washington Higher Education Telecommunications System), computer-assisted instruction, and other methodologies were recommended as considerations in keeping students and faculty informed of library resources and services, and of location, access and use of library materials and services. Because of funding limitations of the past and possible future fiscal constraints, the Task Force also included recommendations and suggestions for supplemental fund-raising and grant-writing activities.

The final report of the Task Force on Library Services at Developing Campuses was completed in early February so that it could be reviewed (prior to the university's biennial budget request to the legislature in June of 1988) by the Academic Senate's Extended University Services committee (for policy development regarding branch campuses), the Associate Provost for Extended University Services' Multi-Campus Implementation Committee, and the University's Biennial Budget Review Committee for Branch Campuses. The result has been the support of branch campus development, particularly for libraries, as one of the highest priorities in the request to the legislature for university funding for the upcoming biennium.

Note

[1] The paper prepared by Barbara Kemp and Maureen Pastine was presented at the fourth Off-campus Library Services Conference, Charleston, South Carolina, and appeared in the 1989 edition of the proceedings.

Accepting the Challenge: Providing Quality Library Services for Distance Education Programs[1]

Anne J. Mathews

When I was asked to address the 1988 Off-campus Library Services Conference, I was asked to comment generally on the role of library services in support of non-traditional learning and specifically about the financial support available through the Office of Library Programs at the U.S. Department of Education. I shall address both of these issues in this article.

In considering the issues pertaining to library services for distance education programs, it is important to have a common "frame of reference"--an agreement on a definition. Just what is distance education? How do each of us define it? From my own experiences, coupled with the numerous articles I have read on the subject, a host of definitions could apply. Most definitions of distance learning include the following characteristics:

- it provides at least occasional interaction with faculty;
- it encourages student independence and individualized study;
- it provides course delivery both on and off campus:
- it is based on student needs (Faibisoff & Willis, 1987, p. 225);
- it frequently includes use of adjunct faculty at a site removed from the host campus.

Throughout this article the terms "distance education" and "off-campus" programs are used interchangeably.

As college costs continue to rise, full-time enrollment at college campuses continues to decline. Yet more and more adults are returning to college to further their education, and distance education is becoming increasingly more important. With the demographics of our educational system changing almost daily, new and innovative approaches to higher education are being developed and implemented.

Quoting Patricia Cross of the Harvard Graduate School of Education, who spoke at Central Michigan University's 1987 Conference on Adult Learning in Higher Education, "The trend is as clear as it is steady. The college campus has burst explosively from its boundaries, and decentralization of learning is a major trend or our times" (Cross,

1987). More and more academic institutions are turning to off-campus programming.

According to the July-August 1988 issue of *The Futurist*, "The learning environment will not be as important to us in the future. Individuals will learn more and more on their own, the places of learning will be more dispersed, and the age at which things are learned will depend on the individual and not on tradition" (Cetron, Rocha & Luckins, 1988).

Some educators suggest that the time is fast approaching when it will be possible for an individual to pursue a college degree without ever setting foot on a college campus. It reminds us that 150 years ago the public library in America was described as the "people's university." We may have come full cycle.

Since the baby-boomers completed their college years, higher education has found itself rapidly changing to meet new needs. In addition, the baby bust which followed the postwar baby boom has reduced the number of young adults enrolled in colleges. However, other factors have come into play that actually increase the need for higher education.

According to George Bates, the Associate Director for Academic Affairs for the Extended Degree Programs of Central Michigan University, the average age of the distance learner or the returning adult learner is actually in the mid-thirties--around 34.5 years old. That, of course, is the average age of the baby boom generation. Just as we saw them depart after their traditional college campus experience and the college enrollment explosion ended, we now find ourselves at the point of picking them up again in our distance education programs.

William Abbott, onetime editor of the World Future Society's *Careers Tomorrow* newsletter suggests that skilled workers will have to attend school at least four times in their lives in order to be totally retrained. He goes on to say in that article that "most workers will probably hold two jobs or go to college on a part-time basis. The need for lifelong learning will be a generally accepted principle" by the year 2001 (Abbott, 1978, p. 99). It appears that no line of work is safe from the demands of lifelong learning. In fact, Abbott believes "It should be clear that the separation between work and education is disappearing"

(Abbott, 1978, p. 101). Furthermore, the rapidly changing job market, coupled with the advances in technology, will necessitate increased training across the board.

In 1982 John Naisbitt told us that "the rapid change ahead means you cannot expect to remain in the same job or profession for life, even if it is an information occupation" (p. 37). In *Megatrends*, Naisbitt identified as one of the trends affecting American life, the shift from interest in the short-term to interest in the long-term. In business, this year's bottom-line is no longer the most important indicator; long-term company growth is. About education he says, "The notion of lifelong learning is already replacing the short-term approach to education, whereby we went to school., graduated, and that was that" (p. 95). Certainly this is one of his predicted trends we are seeing played out.

How is the changing face of higher education affecting library services? As new approaches to higher education are being developed, are new approaches to library services being developed as well?

One positive aspect of the focus on new approaches in higher education is that it may force the library profession to become more proactive about its activities. Think about the following questions: What is the most important service the library is providing off-campus programs? Ten years ago, was it offering that service? To the extend that libraries are providing adequate resources and services to off-campus programs, they are being integrated into the distance education program. But, if libraries are to be a truly integral part of distance learning they must critically assess the quality of their programs and services.

If distance educators accept the concept of lifelong learning and the need for acquiring the skills to "learn how to learn" as goals to be achieved, then they will have to devote increasing energy to helping students acquire effective critical thinking skills, including those in the use of libraries and information. Distance educators will have to offer independent learning activities and projects that encourage learners to exploit the resources and services of libraries within their own communities. The role of resource providers and facilitators (read that, librarians) will become increasingly more important to distance education.

However, do those who plan distance learning activities--conferences, curricula, etc.--consider the role of the library, and include librarians, in their planning? The literature I have explored in sources outside the library field contains few references to library services as a major component to support off-campus programs. This scarcity of information suggests that librarians are not considered major players.

As Theodore Roszak suggested in *The Cult of Information* (1986, p. 172-173), public libraries may be the missing link in the information age--in fact, they may be by-passed completely! I wonder if this is a danger for academic libraries as well? What are libraries and librarians doing to further their role in support of distance education? In fact, do libraries play an important role in ensuring that distance learning students receive a quality education? If so, how, and how do we know? What is the concept of the library in relationship to these changing roles and emerging priorities in distance education? How can we determine the effectiveness of current and future library programs? Or in other words, how do we determine the quality of our library programs and services?

We start to determine quality by asking the right questions. But it is up to us to identify those questions. For example, what is a quality program? or service? and by whose standards? What do we mean when we talk about quality? Which takes me back in my thinking to Robert Pirsig's *Zen and the Art of Motorcycle Maintenance*. Pirsig says that quality is a concept that cannot be defined and cannot be measured. It is something we seek consciously in our many endeavors. It is, if we are talented, persistent and lucky, an experience that we manage to achieve at one time or another in a particular aspect of our lives. It is something that we brush up against occasionally and we most always recognize and appreciate whether it is in the form of a fine symphony or an excellent motor tune up (Pirsig, 1985, p. 167-190). To that last sentence I would add "or good library services."

What can and should we do to ensure quality in our off-campus library services programs based on the needs of the students and within the resources available?

To stimulate your further thinking, the following questions on program planning and evaluation may help generate other questions about the future of library services for distance education.

• What are the current perceptions and emerging priorities in

distance education in the institution?
- What is the concept of the library in relationship to these priorities?
- Does the library have access to the necessary background information--demographic, socioeconomic, and curricular--to develop and evaluate a plan of action?
- How does the library contribute to student learning? How can it better contribute?
- What are the roles and responsibilities of the librarian? Do they need to change and if so, how?
- How effectively do students use the library's services and resources to meet class objectives? Use those of other libraries?
- Does the library need to cooperate with other libraries in order to offer quality services?
- What segments of the distance education population are being reached by existing services? How?
- What plan of action will bring about quality services to support distance learning? How can this plan be developed? Implemented? Evaluated?
- How can the library get key people in the institution to support this plan?
- What criteria can be used to determine the effectiveness of this plan of action? How will these criteria be applied?
- To what extent are the library's program objectives being met?

We can't know what impact we are making or why that impact is important unless there are data to support the statements. The data are essential in helping to make a case for the importance of the library program; developing a research base is extremely important.

For instance, research is needed on the use of telecommunications for the delivery of services. Again, referring to the July-August 1988 issue of *The Futurist*, the authors predict that by the late 1990's, computers will provide access to all the card catalogs of the world's libraries; and that 70% of U.S. homes will have computers by 2001, compared with only 18% today. And, more than three-fourth's of those computers will be equipped to permit communication via networks (Cetron, 1988, p. 30). Given the increased use of telecommunications to provide distance learning, we can predict that library networking and resource sharing will become even more necessary to ensure quality programs and services.

In the book, *Mastering Change*, Leon Martel writes that "the best way to anticipate the future is to understand change" (Martel, 1986, p. 11). As our educational needs evolve, it is no longer possible to solve today's problems with yesterday's solutions. What worked last year won't work this semester. We can either bemoan this fact or use it to find new answers, new solutions and new ideas for providing quality library programs and services. However, quality does not come easily and more often than not it comes at great expense. It requires dedication, effort, and innovation. It also requires money.

Money does not ensure quality. But it allows us to try out innovative approaches or to test untried theories, one of which might make an important contribution to improving the quality of library services for off-campus programs.

The second topic I was asked to address concerns some of the resource possibilities available through the U.S. Department of Education's Office of Library Programs.

The Office of Library Programs under the authority of the Library Services and Construction Act (LSCA) and Title II of the Higher Education Act (HEA II) administers a $138 million program that supports libraries throughout the Nation. Most of this money is earmarked for public and academic libraries. The focus of these programs is to support projects designed to strengthen and upgrade the quality, resources, and services of our Nation's libraries.

Four of those programs have particular relevance to academic library needs and interests. They are:

• the Library Career Training Program, and
• the Library Research and Demonstration Program, both of which make up Title II-B of the Higher Education Act;
• the College Library Technology and Cooperation Grants Program, which is Title II-D of the same act; and
• the Interlibrary Cooperation and Resource Sharing Program which is Title III of the Library Services and Construction Act.

All of the grants awarded through Title II of the Higher Education Act are discretionary and are administered directly by the Office of Library Programs. To ensure equitable treatment, a peer review process is used to evaluate all applications.

Through HEA II-B, the Library Career Training Program awards grants to institutions of higher education and other library organizations to assist in the training of individuals in librarianship and to establish, develop, and expand programs of library and information science. Grantees may use these funds for fellowships, traineeships, and institutes.

In the summer of 1988, the Office of Library Programs awarded twenty-three grants, totalling $410,000 to support twenty-three fellowships and three institutes. Many of the projects funded provide training and retraining of library personnel in areas of specialization where there are currently shortages, such as school media, children's and young adult services, science reference, and cataloging.

Other projects will support institutes to train or retrain library personnel in new techniques of information acquisition, transfer, and communication technology, and to increase excellence in library leadership through advanced training in library management and evaluation.

For example, the School of Library and Information Science at the University of Wisconsin, Milwaukee received a $26,909 grant to fund the Urban Library Management Institute to prepare middle managers to manage changes affecting libraries. The one-week institute is designed to give participants from urban academic and public libraries insights into emerging fiscal, demographic, educational, technological, and cultural trends affecting the development and delivery of library services into the twenty-first century.

The other part of HEA II-B, the Library Research and Demonstration Program, provides grants to institutions of higher education and other public and private organizations for research and demonstration projects pertaining to library improvement, training in librarianship, and for the dissemination of information resulting from these projects.

This past year, we received 49 applications requesting a total of $4.2 million; unfortunately, we had only $309,000 to award. Of those 49 applications, 26 were eligible for review, and 5 of those were ultimately funded.

One of our fiscal year 1988 grant recipients was Clarion State University. Their research centered on: What do rural people think about their public libraries? What are the information needs of rural Americans? And, to what extent do rural public libraries meet the information needs of their users? Based on these findings, Clarion State is developing and disseminating training materials for rural public librarians to help them become more efficient in serving their constituencies. I mention this because I think distance learning students may be one of their "new" constituencies.

Every year the Secretary of Education establishes priorities for research. For 1989, the first priority addresses the library's role-- educational, cultural, and intellectual--in relation to other educational institutions.

The second priority focuses on what we need to know about the library user, non-user, and potential user in order to assess the quality of service and resources and the extent to which the information needs of the community are being met.

The third priority is directed at identifying the potential effects of new technologies on user access to information, indicators of access to information, and the extent to which format affects access and use of information.

The fourth priority for 1989 will study the economics of libraries and the factors that influence library funding.

The third funding program, the College Library Technology and Cooperation Grants Program, HEA II-D, is the newest program and potentially the most competitive one. The purpose of this grants program is to encourage the development of exemplary uses of technological equipment in libraries of institutions of higher education.

There are four type of grants awarded. Authorized activities for all four types of grants include:

- buying access to networks,
- acquiring additional equipment and supplies that will assist in achieving the purpose of the project,
- paying staff,
- paying for telecommunications expenses,
- evaluating the project, and
- disseminating information about the project.

The minimum grant given in any of the four categories is $15,000 and projects are funded for up to a three-year period. Applicants are required to spend not less than one-third of the total grant award from funds other than those received under HEA II-D. For example, if a library received the minimum $15,000 award, the institution would have to match that amount with $5,000.

In the first category, *Networking*, institutions of higher education may apply to plan, develop, acquire, install, maintain or replace technological equipment necessary to participate in networks for sharing library resources. This past year most applicants requested support to purchase the equipment necessary to participate in OCLC or a regional network to facilitate interlibrary loan and to contribute their records.

Secondly, *Combinations of Institutions* of higher education may apply for Combination grants to establish and strengthen joint-use library facilities, resources, or equipment. Many applicants requested funds to create shared online catalogs and acquisitions programs; to strengthen existing shared systems through reconversion of records; and, to establish new levels of cooperation either regionally or through the coordination of specialized subject area collections.

For *Services to Institutions* grants, public or private nonprofit organizations which provide library and information services to institutions of higher education on a formal cooperative basis may apply to establish, develop, or expand programs or projects that improve information services to institutions of higher education. Under this category, public libraries, state library administrative agencies and special libraries applied mostly to improve and expand access to materials via interlibrary loan to the institutions in their regions; to create dial-up access to special collection indices to support the academic programs of the institutions they serve; and to create broad-based regional resource centers for the institutions in their area.

And finally, for *Research and Demonstration* grants, institutions of higher education may apply to conduct research or demonstration projects to meet specialized national or regional needs in utilizing technology to enhance library information sciences.

The fiscal year 1988 applications ran the gamut of innovative ideas and approaches, including: the improvement of reference services via remote access to CD-ROM databases; increasing the ability of end-users to decipher the myriad of computerized information sources by creating full service, integrated library workstations using advanced function stations, optical disc storage and expert system components; behavioral studies of information seekers using computers as a means of developing improved programs for ease of use, precision and output; improvement of the speed of delivery of interlibrary loan items via telefacsimile or other means; intelligent character recognition to facilitate reconversion efforts; and ideas for uses of satellite equipment to capture the transmission of information from around the globe to strengthen and create new academic programs.

HEA, Title II-D was authorized by Congress for the first time in fiscal year 1988 with an appropriation of $3.59 million. Three hundred thirty applications were received requesting almost $27 million. A total of 45 proposals were funded with average grants ranging from $24,000 in the Services to Institutions category to $115,000 in Research and Demonstration.

The fourth source of funding in the Office of Library Programs is Title III of the Library Services and Construction Act--LSCA-- which supports interlibrary cooperation and resource sharing. Unlike the Higher Education Act funds just mentioned, these LSCA funds are distributed directly to the States through formula grants and the State library agency becomes responsible for their administration. In fiscal year 1988 the States received $18.2 million for Title III purposes. Congress recently appropriated $19,102,000 in funding for fiscal year 1989.

The purpose of Title III is to allow the States to develop, establish, expand or operate local, State, regional and interstate cooperative library networks among public, academic, school and special libraries. The State library agencies may fund three types of activities:

• planning for cooperative library networks;
• establishing, expanding, and operating library networks; and
• planning for Statewide resource sharing.

How each State uses its Title III allotment depends on its needs and long-range plan and annual program; however, many States do run grant competitions. Since States manage their grant competitions differently, it would be difficult to explore subgranting practices without getting into specifics--guidelines, criteria, funding periods, and application procedures--of individual States. To find out whether or not a State offers grant competitions for LSCA, Title III funds, contact the State librarian or the LSCA officer at the State library agency.

It is imperative that libraries provide quality services. As new approaches to distance education are developed, new approaches to library services must also be developed. The Office of Library Programs can provide some funding for innovation, but librarians must provide the innovative ideas. Charting a course for the future of library services to off-campus programs is a major responsibility and a great challenge -- one librarians must accept.

References

Abbott, W. (1980). Beating Unemployment through Education. In E. Cornish (Ed.), *1999: The World of Tomorrow*. Washington, D.C.: World Future Society.

Cetron, M. J., Rocha, W. & Luckins, R. (1988). Into the 21st Century: Long Term Trends Affecting the United States. *The Futurist, 22*(4), 33.

Cross, K. P. (June 19, 1987). *Adult Learners in Higher Education: Planning for Excellence.* Paper presented at the Central Michigan University Conference on Adult Learners in Higher Education, Mt. Pleasant, MI.

Faibisoff, S. G. & Willis, D. J. (1987). Distance Education: Definition and Overview. *Journal of Education for Library and Information Science, 27*(4), 225.

Martel, L. (1986). *Mastering Change: The Key to Business Success.* New York: Simon and Schuster.

Naisbitt, J. (1982). *Megatrends: Ten New Directions Transforming Our Lives.* New York: Warner.

Pirsig, R. (1985). *Zen and the Art of Motorcycle Maintenance.* New York: Bantam.

Roszak, T. (1986). *The Cult of Information: the Folklore of Computers and the True Art of Thinking.* New York: Pantheon.

Note

[1] Dr. Mathews' paper was presented at the fourth Off-campus Library Services Conference, Charleston, South Carolina, and appeared in the 1989 edition of the conference proceedings.

The Ties That Bind:
Organizational Structure of Off-campus Libraries[1]

Nancy J. Burich

As declining enrollments approach institutions of higher education, there is increasing competition for students. Institutions have tried a variety of approaches to recruit students. In some cases, separate institutions may join together to form one unit. Examples of this type of coalition include the University of California (at Los Angeles, Berkeley, Irving, Davis, Riverside, San Diego, Santa Barbara, and Santa Cruz), the State University of New York (at Albany, Binghamton, Buffalo, and Stony Brook), and the University of Missouri (at Columbia, Kansas City, Rolla, and St. Louis). In this type of organization, each "branch" or "off-campus" unit consists of a separate campus offering a full range of degree programs, a wide variety of services, and a separate academic library. The organization and administration of these libraries do not differ significantly from academic libraries of institutions having a single geographic location.

However, there is another approach to recruiting students which differs significantly from traditional academic models. This is to establish an off-campus center in a metropolitan area which is otherwise not served by an academic institution. The center has as its main goal the recruitment of adult students--a population usually not served by an academic institution. A facility is acquired to house classes and s small administrative staff. Faculty are supplied by the main campus. Because most students are adults, services are minimal. There may be a library, but its facilities and staff are limited. The University of Kansas Regents Center is one such off-campus center. It is located in the Kansas City metropolitan area, forty miles from the main campus in Lawrence, Kansas. It is housed in a renovated elementary school building, and the library occupies the old gymnasium. The Regents Center will serve as a model for comments about the organizational structure of this type of off-campus center for remote education.

The typical Regents Center student has a family as well as regular employment. This person is usually a woman (women outnumber men three to one), and the average age is thirty-five. To most students, time is more important than money because they have more of the latter than the former. These students are highly motivated, having given up something to attend classes. In addition, being experienced consumers, they want their money's worth from classes. However, they are isolated from on-campus student services, including the academic library. Public libraries which may be near the off-campus center usually cannot meet all research and reserve needs of these students. Therefore, the off-campus center must provide services to support adequately the courses and degrees offered there. Because of the limited size of the center library, it must rely on the main campus library for many technical and public service operations. Because is likely that the needs of the center library will have an impact on all main library departments, center personnel must be able to develop and maintain close working relationships with all campus library departments.

The personnel of an off-campus library must work with a unique and complex organizational structure. The 1982 "Guidelines for Extended Campus Library Services" specify as personnel, "Persons with the capacity and skills to identify needs and respond to them flexibly and creatively" (Association of College and Research Libraries). The responsibilities of the center librarian separate her from other academic librarians and have implications for education, training, and recruitment. The reasons for needing these characteristics become clear after analyzing the ties which bind such an off-campus library.

In a recent editorial, Charles Martel wrote, "In libraries, the lines of authority and responsibility create a structure that governs (1) who sets the goals, (2) how resources are allocated, (3) who makes decisions about what, (4) who evaluates, (5) who is to do what, and (6) what means are to be used" (Martel, 1986). In most academic libraries, the organizational structure governs in a straightforward manner. At the University of Kansas, the Vice Chancellor for Academic Affairs oversees the library, the Dean of Libraries oversees Assistant Deans who oversee Technical Service and Public Service departments. Graphically, the organization chart looks like this:

Figure 1. Organization chart for the University of Kansas Libraries.

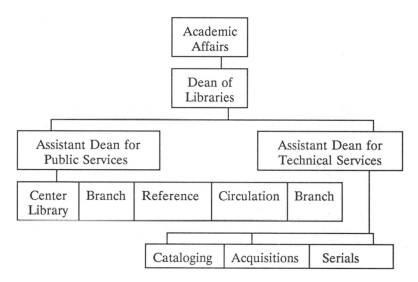

The Regents Center itself has similar ties to the main campus through Academic Affairs, and there is a Center Director who administers the facility. In addition, there are student services, including the library. The Regents Center organization has the following configuration:

Figure 2. Regents Center organization chart

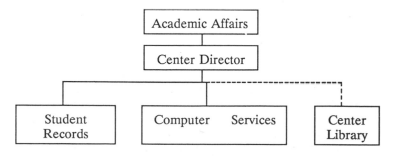

In Figures 1 and 2, solid lines represent authority and responsibility while broken lines represent responsiveness which links the library to the Center. Both the libraries and the Center provide elements in the organizational structure of the Center library which are essential to the effective delivery of off-campus library services. The main library provides administrative leadership within the context of institution-wide priorities. It establishes an operational framework of policies and procedures. It allocates the budget for equipment, staff, and materials. It provides centralized technical services including systems and technology, acquisitions, cataloging, and serials. Finally, the campus provides colleagues with whom an off-campus librarian can exchange ideas, discuss problems, and achieve professional development. Because of the isolation of the off-campus facility, its reliance on campus departments for essential operations, and the demand made on every department in the main library, the Center librarian must carefully nurture responsiveness throughout the library organization. In many respects, the closest colleagues may be other branch librarians. Though the organization, procedures, and specifics of daily operation may be quite different, a branch librarian still shares many common experiences with an off-campus colleague. However, the distance from campus and the absence of daily contact make responsiveness and close ties with campus colleagues difficult to achieve and maintain.

Responsiveness here means more than providing the services requested. It implies an understanding that even though the Center library is a part of the library system, its priorities and its policies and procedures often differ from those on campus. Through a slow process, each main library department must be educated to recognize that the Center Library is different, that it does not necessarily fit the pattern established by other branches. Thus the Center Library orders and acquires its own books, it receives and checks-in its own serials, and it requires precedence in cataloging its materials. Similarly, the public services which it offers often differ from campus practices. Even the days and hours of operation are different from those on campus.

Because the off-campus library is unique, it is essential that the library administration recognize and support its unparalleled position. Such support should include a willingness to allow the Center librarian to explore all avenues that may lead to improved library services. This will almost certainly mean greater freedom for the Center librarian than accorded to other branch librarians. Once such a policy has been established by the library administration, it is likely that all library personnel will adopt it. Without such administrative support, cooperation or responsiveness may be sporadic or non-existent, disrupting Center library operation.

The Regents Center plays an important part in providing library services. First, it determines the quality and quantity of library facilities. Facilities mean more than book stacks, index tables, and service desks. There must be adequate study space. Students with families may want to escape the activities at home and seek a quiet place to study at the Center. Others may want to meet informally to discuss homework with classmates. Therefore, the Center needs to provide both kinds of study space--individual, and quiet areas, and group discussion areas. In addition, the Center must provide communication capabilities and security for automated library systems. Because the Center library contains only a small portion of campus collections, it must borrow materials as they are needed from campus. Often, the Center transports these materials from campus as well as faculty and supplies. The timely (and preferably daily) exchange of information and materials is essential for effective library services. Because the main library is not equipped for such service, the Center's library must look to the Center for reliable transport. Finally, since the Center offers only a selection of courses and degree programs which are available on campus, the curriculum determines the library's collection development policy. Plans to add or delete programs must be communicated to the librarian with sufficient lead time so that the collections on campus and at the Center can be surveyed to determine whether they can support the changes planned. Then a coordinated acquisitions program can be initiated to assure that materials and services are available when courses are taught. It should never be assumed that this information will be forwarded to the librarian automatically. The librarian must take the initiative and seek information through informal talks with faculty and Center administrative personnel is as important as good relations within the main library.

It is a difficult task to balance the goals and expectations of the campus library and those of the off-campus Center and its library. For example, the Center may be expanding programs as it seeks to attract new students, while declining or stable enrollments on campus strictly limit resources available for maintaining current services or for expanding them. Further, as the newest and smallest branch, its needs rank low in the library's over-all budgetary priorities. Ironically, it may be the enrollments generated off-campus which provide any increases in resources for campus programs. Because of this conflict, the librarian must have the freedom and the encouragement of the library administration to initiate and develop whatever services and collections are necessary to meet changing student needs. This is the time when the Center library must go its own way, developing and fitting non-traditional services to the needs of non-traditional students. But how does the off-campus library compete with campus needs which are older than the Center itself? How can the librarian secure funding to provide library services for new courses and programs during times of tight budgets? If lobbying efforts with library administrators and with faculty members prove ineffective, the most logical place to turn is to the Center. After all, without library collections and services, Center degree programs may lose accreditation and most of their students. Therefore, it is in the best interests of the Center to provide whatever aid it can to the library.

Figure 3. Organization chart for the Regents Center and the Libraries.

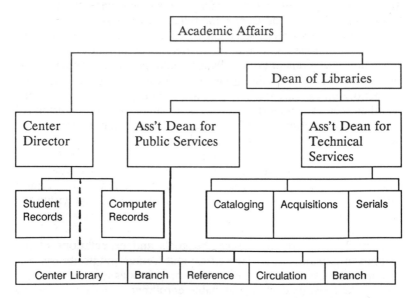

However, once the Center library has received budgetary support from another agency, ties which once were concerned with responsiveness change to those of authority and responsibility. For example, a staff position provided by the Center for the library will cause personnel ambiguities. Who controls how the individual's time will be spent, or evaluates raises and promotions? Similar questions arise concerning any expenditure which is shared. Someone must assume responsibility and, therefore, control By accepting outside funding, no matter how worthy or necessary the cause, the Center librarian acquires a second boss. Loyalties and priorities become split. The Center librarian must be responsive to both the library and to the Center while maintaining the integrity of Center library operations.

Even though ties to the main library are strong and there exists the flexibility to provide library services by whatever means practical, the librarian must have the freedom to initiate and establish additional ties. The main campus library probably is too far away for patrons to make the trip to use collections and services regularly. Therefore, ties must exist with other metropolitan area libraries. Ideally, the off-campus student should have access to all area networks and consortia. In the absence of such cooperative groups, ties have been established including public, private, community college, and special libraries. Such cooperation is usually most welcome since it means that the network or individual library will gain access to academic library materials it would otherwise lack. Conversely, the academic community will have access to more popular and specialized materials which it usually will not acquire. However, when such ties are established, it must be determined whether the Center library or the parent institution will be involved. The question is whether the off-campus library or the main library's interlibrary loan office is better able to handle exchanges of materials with metropolitan area libraries.

No matter how many agreements are initiated, the off-campus student will certainly use his public library. There the student will hope to find reference materials and assistance, serial publications, government documents, and reserve readings. Even though a cooperative agreement exists between the Center library and the local public library, and even though the student may already be paying taxes to support the public library and, therefore, have every right to use its resources, the Center librarian can facilitate such use. It is useful to supply reading lists and to inform public library personnel about changes in the curriculum so that they are prepared for questions and requests for materials. On the surface, this benefits only the public library. However, any type of cooperation can help the Center library, especially when the result is to improve library services to students--the primary goal of the library. If the student is unable to draw on area library resources directly by driving to the library and checking out materials, the quality of education will suffer, and the student will be frustrated because he lacks access to necessary materials. It is likely that this frustration will be laid before the Center librarian--exactly where it belongs. The goal should be to access all county and area library resources. Each linkage is important; the more ties which can be established the better. The organizational chart for this configuration is as follows.

Figure 4. Organization chart for Regents Center Library and its ties.

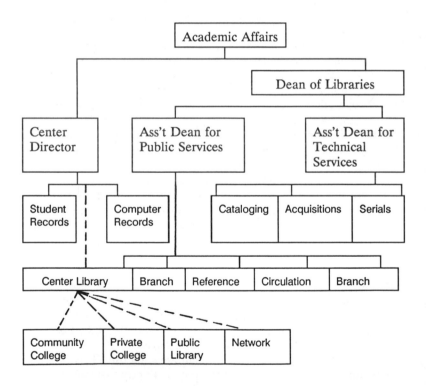

Thus, the off-campus librarian is literally in the middle juggling and grappling with a multitude of ties, both formal and informal, which insure the widest possible variety of services and collections for students, Such words as diplomatic, resourceful, flexible, coordinator, facilitator, and effective communicator must apply to the librarian. All these attributes must be used in a continuous effort to promote the off-campus library in the community. This is an activity that is usually unfamiliar to an on-campus librarian, and especially to branch librarians. Once again, this responsibility illustrates the role which ties play in the daily operation of an off-campus library.

The off-campus librarian has responsibilities which are unique among academic librarians. In one respect, the Center exists in isolation. It does not have extensive facilities, permanent faculties, vast bureaucracies, boosters or alumni, or separate resources. Its locale does not depend on it for jobs and economic well-being. These are conditions which exist on most campuses. Rather, the Center exists as long as it benefits the parent institution. If it becomes a liability or drains resources from campus operations, it can be closed. Being fully aware of this fact, the Center librarian must do whatever possible to promote the Center as well as the library. Students must be attracted to the Center and retained.   Services, such as the library, are important.   Therefore, library employees must recognize that the Center library is a service unit.   It is the student who determines collections, goals, and services. The Center library must do everything it can to facilitate the learning process and to make using the library a pleasant experience.

The Center librarian must become adept at recognizing the needs of faculty and students.   Then the librarian must survey the resources available to meet them. The next step is to implement access to these resources by initiating ties with various other libraries. Finally, the librarian manipulates the ties with various agencies to provide the best library resources and services possible. The organizational structure of the off-campus library determines the qualities necessary in its librarian, who is vital to the success of off-campus education.

References

Association of College and Research Libraries.   Standards and Accreditation Committee. (1982).   Guidelines for extended campus library services. *College and Research Libraries News*, *43*, 86-88.

Martel, C. (1986). Editorial: Participative management. *College and Research Libraries*, *47*, 5-6.

Note

[1] The paper prepared by Ms. Burich was presented at the third Off-campus Library Services Conference, Reno, Nevada, and appeared in the 1987 edition of the conference proceedings.

Notes About the Contributors

William Aguilar was Director of the Burritt Library at Central Connecticut State University in 1987. He now serves as University Librarian at California State University at San Bernardino and was co-editor of the Spring, 1991 *Library Trends* issue devoted to off-campus library services.

Stephanie Rogers Bangert is the Director of the Saint Mary's College Library in Moraga, California.

Nancy J. Burich is Regents Center Librarian at the University of Kansas at Overland Park.

Geneva L. Bush is a Senior Librarian of the University of South Alabama.

Eileen Chalfoun is Coordinator of Research and Information Services for the Community College of Vermont.

John F. Cook is Dean of Business and Public Management at the State University of New York College of Technology at Utica/Rome.

Mary Lou Wranesh Cook is Associate Professor of Nursing at the State University of New York College of Technology at Utica/Rome.

Christine Crocker was until recently the Reader Services Librarian at Deakin University in Geelong, Victoria, Australia. She is now the University Librarian at the University of Tasmania.

James A. Damico is Director of Libraries at the University of South Alabama.

Raymond K. Fisher is Librarian in the School of Continuing Studies at the University of Birmingham, United Kingdom.

Antoinette M. Kania is Dean of Libraries for the Suffolk Community College, a unit of the State University of New York.

Marie Kascus is Serials Librarian at Burritt Library at Central Connecticut State University and was a co-editor of the Spring, 1991 *Library Trends* issue devoted to off-campus library services.

Patricia M. Kelley is Assistant University Librarian for Programs and Services at the George Washington University.

Barbara E. Kemp was Head, Humanities and Social Sciences and Library Instruction at Washington State University in 1989. She now serves as Lehman Librarian at the Columbia University Libraries.

Barton M. Lessin is Assistant Dean of Libraries at Wayne State University. While at Central Michigan University Libraries (1979-1989) he directed that institution's off-campus library support program and was responsible for the development and implementation of the Off-campus Library Services Conference. He serves as the first elected chair of the Association of Research Libraries Extended Campus Library Services Section.

Dennis Lindberg was Director of Information and Research Services for the Vermont State Colleges in 1987. He is now Executive Vice President of Chicago West Pullman Corporation of Cincinnati, Ohio.

H. Maynard Lowry is Director of the University Library at Loma Linda University, Riverside, California.

Terrence J. MacTaggart is Chancellor of the University of Wisconsin-Superior.

Anne J. Mathews is Director of the Office of Library Programs at the United States Department of Education.

Brian Nielsen is Assistant University Librarian for Branch Libraries and Information Services Technology at Northwestern University.

Maureen Pastine was Director of Libraries at Washington State University in 1989. She now serves at Director of the Central University Libraries at Southern Methodist University.

Mary Joyce Pickett was Schaffner Project Librarian at Northwestern University in Chicago, Illinois when her article was prepared. She is now Director of Library Services at Illinois Benedictine College.

Richard H. Potter is Associate Director of the Central Michigan University Institute for Personal and Career Development.

Alexander L. Slade is Coordinator of Extension Library Services for the University Library of the University of Victoria, Victoria, British Columbia, Canada.

Susan Swords Steffen is Head of the Joseph Schaffner Library at Northwestern University in Chicago, Illinois.

John W. Weatherford is Emeritus Director of the Central Michigan University Libraries.

Name Index

Subject Index

Accreditation, role of, 78-79
Accreditation standards, 66-74. *See also* Connecticut licensure, 85-93
Accreditor's perspective: adequate services, 80-81; development of off-campus library services, 81-82; of off-campus library programs, 77-84; off-campus library services, 79-80; renaissance in off-campus library services, 82-84; role of accreditation, 78-79
Adequate services, 80-81
Australia. *See* Off-campus library services in Australia, 122-148
Bibliographic instruction, 13, 21, 51-52, 138-139, 144-145
Branch operations, 17-19. *See also* Washington State University
Case studies. *See* Instructional resources
Central Michigan University off-campus library services: home collection usage, 2; incremental funding model, 2-3; instructional resources support, 116-120; organizational structure, 4; program assumptions, 1-2
Circulation, 12-13
Classification of off-campus library services, 161-170
Collection development, 27, 57-58
Community College of Vermont: computerized resource file, 32-33; degree planning seminar, 31; guide to use of resources, 30-31; reference collections, 33; self-reliant learner, 30. *See also* Vermont State Colleges
Computer software. *See* Instructional resources
Connecticut licensure and accreditation regulation: comparison of regulations, 87-89; enrollment trends, 85-86; impact of regulations on two institutions, 91-92; in-state and out-of-state programs, 89-90; overview, 85; reasons for non-compliance, 90-91
Database searching, 13, 53-55
Deakin University, 127-130
Development of off-campus library services, 81-82
Distance learning characteristics, 209
Document delivery, 3, 9, 42-43, 194
England. *See* Separate library collections, 149-160
Evaluation of library services, 13-15
Faculty development. *See* Instructional resources
Faculty participation at Northwestern University, 193
Faculty perspectives regarding educational support off-campus: conclusions of survey, 112; format of survey employed, 106-107; library services, 110; results of survey, 107-111
Incremental cost structure, 2-3